LifeLight

TAKING THE CHURCH OUTSIDE THE WALLS

LifeLight

TAKING THE CHURCH OUTSIDE THE WALLS

ALAN GREENE

THRONE
PUBLISHING GROUP

Responses to *LifeLight: Taking the Church Outside the Walls*

"In *Taking the Church Outside the Walls* businessman turned evangelist Alan Greene describes his own spiritual journey and how he and his wife Vicki launched the LifeLight festivals. The result is a very compelling challenge to all Jesus followers to not to just do church but become the church by being intentional in taking the light of the Good News of Jesus Christ into a dark world. God is in the business of changing lives and drawing people to Himself and He expects us to cooperate with Him in that mission by taking church out into the marketplace. This is a very timely book that will shake up Jesus followers and churches out of their passivity."

— Kevin Palau, President, Luis Palau Association

"It's far too common for Jesus followers to get comfortable doing church on Sundays resulting in church goers becoming disengaged from their neighbors and the "un-churched." In *Taking the Church Outside the Walls* Alan Greene describes his own personal wake-up call that there will be no evangelism in heaven and that God expects us to join Him now in drawing people to Himself. That reality led Alan and his wife Vicki to launch the LifeLight festivals that annually help churches and Christians reach thousands with the life changing Good News of Jesus Christ. In doing so Alan and Vicki and many others have discovered the reality and meaning in their lives that was missing by playing church."

—David L. Jones, Vice President of Corporate Affairs, Luis Palau Association

"*Taking the Church Outside the Walls* is a manifesto of what can be accomplished when you hear and obey that quiet voice of the Holy Spirit inside your heart, nudging you to act. The reason that taking the Gospel outside of our church walls works so well is that God never intended for us to limit our vision. This book will inspire you to search deep inside your soul to discover the big vision God has for you in your future."

— Dick Jenkins, Dick Jenkins Consulting

"This is our favorite music festival of the year!"

— Jon & Sherry Rivers, 20 The Countdown Magazine

"Alan Greene's passionate heart for the least, the last and the lost is authentic and contagious. He is a powerful communicator whose actions mirror his words. Alan eagerly and faithfully enters God's vineyard daily knowing that the fields are white for the harvest. I am honored to be considered his friend and co-laborer."

— Bob Thompson, Executive Director,
Christian Festival Association

"I am pleased to recommend *Taking the Church Outside the Walls*. It has been my joy to have had a small part in the lives of Alan & Vicki Greene and the LifeLight miracle from the beginning of this great ministry. What impresses me most about this book is how Alan & Vicki have allowed the Lord to speak to them and to lead them through their journey—this is not a book of fiction—this is how I have watched them live. I believe you will be inspired to live out your own life being led by the Lord into an adventure that will take your life outside of the church and allowing your light to shine in a dark world."

— Pastor Ron Traub, South Dakota District Assembly of God

"I've been in ministry for 31 years, traveled the country, and have been to countless festivals. In all the festivals I have been to, there is a special anointing on LifeLight. Alan and Vicki Greene have hearts for ministry and for the core of the Gospel. They have provided a festival where thousands and thousands have received Christ. This is something historic in South Dakota to see so many people gather for the name of Jesus, to unify churches, to glorify Christ and to proclaim the Gospel."

— Bob Lenz, Founder and Speaker of Life Promotions and Lifest

"*Taking the Church Outside the Walls* is the compelling and amazing story of what God can do through two people who are totally sold out to Him. When God gave Alan and Vicki Greene the vision for LifeLight, no one would have guessed that it would become the largest festival of its kind in the world. My wife, Kimberley, and I have witnessed firsthand the 'Light of Life' shared with literally hundreds of thousands of people each and every year. Anyone who wants to be encouraged about the work of Christ in the culture needs to read this book."

— Senator John Thune (SD)

"Just like God's love, this book is all about reaching souls and expanding His Kingdom. There is no doubt, Jesus has long arms and He knows no borders! When Christ saved Alan & Vicki Greene, the Spirit ignited within them a Jabez-like prayer and vision to take the Gospel beyond the walls of the Church. As a result, LifeLight was fanned into flame. May the Light of Life use this book to kindle our hearts to pray, 'Oh that You would bless me/us indeed and enlarge my/our border(s).'"

— Pastor Michael Brandt, Director of Shepherding the Shepherds

"You can't help but be awestruck while reading *Taking the Church Outside the Walls* at how much God loves us. Alan Greene has done an incredible job of being faithful to keep a watchful eye for God blessings in his life. This book will motivate you to thank God for his many blessings...even when those blessings come from a place and time that was never in your heart, prayers or your best guess. It's easy to read a book written by a man you have watched walk with God in unequivocal faith. Be prepared…after reading just a few chapters, you will be awestruck at how God works. I guarantee there is a message in this book for anyone who reads it!!"

— Al Denson, Christian Recording Artist

ISBN: 978-0-9895244-7-6

Printed in the United States of America.
Cover design by Anneli Anderson
Book design by Tim Murray, paperbackdesign.com/books

Throne Publishing Group
220 S. Phillips Ave.
Sioux Falls, SD 57104
thronepg.com

For our precious grandchildren—gifts of God:
Shade, Kyera, Taylie, and Alayah

And in memory of my late mother, though she died long before the ministry grew into what it is today, she was the creative writer, dreamer, and visionary who gave constant encouragement and love to me and our family.

Contents

Foreword

The first time I met Alan Greene face-to-face, I wondered if he was crazy.

And I don't mean "crazy" as some diluted vernacular to explain how he was intense, bizarre, or a person who didn't follow convention.

I was examining his mannerisms as if he was literally insane.

Or, at least, trending toward that status as he stared at me with eyes that didn't seem to blink and appeared to grow wider as he spoke about staging a Christian Music Festival on the county fairgrounds because God told him to.

You have to understand, I was apprehensive about such claims. At the time, I was working as a pop culture reporter and columnist at the daily newspaper in Sioux Falls, South Dakota, and as the paper's resident outlier, my job often meant intersecting with unstable people who just had to tell me about their encounters with "celebrities," why a certain band was secretly genius, or how God was speaking to them through movies, books, or the red stone quarries that were common to the region. So when Alan was laying out a festival plan that wasn't fully formed and missing key components, I cast him as a part of the local crackpot crew.

Of course, I was wrong.

That summer of 2001, Alan guided LifeLight to new heights as this Christian music festival drew 10,000 people to the county fairgrounds. No one entrenched in the local scene could have predicted that success for something that was a simple parking lot concert 12 months earlier, which is probably why most of the local scenesters, arts peers, and regional media kind of ignored LifeLight as some strange anomaly powered by a chorus of believers and not much else. At first, I was standing among the skeptics. I wasn't there to see the 2001 festival, eschewing the LifeLight assignment to cover a sloppy rock music festival 60 miles north. My perspective soon changed, as did LifeLight, growing into the largest music festival most of America doesn't realize exists.

Through my years in Sioux Falls, I met with Alan often, listening to how his ministry kept defying failure by last minute windfalls bordering on miracles and how he wanted to tear down the divisions that segregate Christian denominations. The more we talked, the more I realized something unique and special was going on with this music festival, and the ministry that played like a rational trailblazer in a Christian culture of archaic habits.

As a journalist, I covered the festival and the ministry with objectivity in mind. As a person, I had some issues with a couple of their religious beliefs—I'm sure they'd say the same about me, a non-dogmatic spiritualist. But as someone who studies popular culture as a way to explain and define society, I was mesmerized by LifeLight. While most music festivals tend to draw a throng of converts who already preach the message they're singing along to, the LifeLight fests always attracted people who didn't fit the Christian mold of neo-evangelicals in the 2000s—non-church-going casual Christians, curious non-believers, music fans with limited religious interest, etc. Sure, there was a considerable pack of believers just waiting to raise their hands to the sky every time Michael W. Smith or Chris Tomlin sang a mere mention of the Lord. They were the choir Alan and others preached to. But when I walked around the LifeLight grounds with an objective eye, I noticed people who weren't there for the faith component, people who just wanted to rock. And though that might seem like a "duh" fact given there were a host of rock acts playing LifeLight, I didn't see that unbiased demographic at the other large scale fests I frequented. LifeLight was drawing the people who weren't supposed to be at a Christian music festival, which is exactly what Alan wanted in his mission to take the church beyond the church walls.

I've always been drawn toward iconoclasts, especially those who tread in pop culture. But there was another reason I found a connection to Alan; I've heard God's voice too.

It spoke to me twice, planting a resonant but subtle voice in the back of my head that offered a sense of calm and enlightenment rarely felt in life. The second message came while I was praying one night, asking for relief for a family member with a painful health condition. I started bargaining, telling God I'd do what was needed of me if the pain and the condition that caused it could be cured. Most of my prayers aren't answered with much more than a feeling. But this time, I heard the response, "Write a book about LifeLight."

It was odd because, well, I didn't want to. Researching, writing, and trying to publish a book about a Christian music festival just didn't fit into my life's plan. But, as Alan says a few times in this book, when God talks, you listen. And then you act in the faith that a greater power knows what you need to do more than you do. So I emailed Alan with that story about my Godly directive. He wasn't surprised. At all. In fact, Alan and his wife Vicki had been talking about how they needed to write a book about their ministry. Synchronicity, it's an amazing thing.

Though this project has been delayed a couple times due to life changes and business developments and has morphed from a journalistic narrative project to a firsthand story told by the man who's been charged to bring LifeLight to the world, it's finally here as another piece of the LifeLight puzzle that's been inspiring people to find some faith since that 2001 festival caused so many of us to turn our heads in wonderment.

Alan Greene is a sane, inspiring man. We were just foolish to doubt him—or maybe Him. Keep that in mind as you read this story about LifeLight's genesis and growth through anecdotes that, at times, feel exaggerated or unreal. It's all truth, told by a man resigned to the fact that there's a greater force guiding him through life.

Robert Morast, Journalist & News Reporter
July 2014

Preface

Flashbacks—I've had a few of them while writing this book.

I see Skillet, Casting Crowns, Newsboys, and countless other acts silhouetted against the flashing lights and feel the pounding bass shake the ground beneath my feet. The buzz of excitement from the crowd around me almost makes the hair on my arms stand on end, in a good way. And the smells of frying funnel cakes interlaced with the tangy, earthy smell of the surrounding alfalfa fields accent the lights and the sound—this is a festival!

Tears well up in my eyes as the music and words spoken reach into hearts and people respond to God in their own way, but also in a unified effort as part of the crowd. One young man is kneeling, squeezing past the legs of those around him to seek God. Across the field, a woman is lifting her hands to the sky, and another's eyes are fixed on the stage as she hangs on every word.

I see myself in that field in my mind's eye. And I recall the stories people have told me over and over about how they felt like God was speaking directly to them, even among the massive crowds.

I know what that feels like. In fact, that's why they are telling me their own stories of encounter. God spoke directly to me. Even when I was only one among thousands.

Over the years, people have asked me, "Why is there not a book about your journey?" Then the questions would turn into divinely inspired directions—people would look at me and say things like, "Alan, I feel like God is saying, 'Write a book.'"

But a book was not exactly on my to-do list. And I never felt like with the busy life that I live I would allow time to commit to the project. However, the pulling to follow that advice started to get stronger, and I would see signs or hints about it everywhere.

I was even at a church as a guest for an ordination, and the speaker, who didn't know me from Adam, said in front of everyone, "I think God is saying that man is supposed to write a book." He followed that statement saying, "I don't know what he does or what it is about, but I saw in my mind a book from that man."

Wow—he got my attention! After that I finally admitted to myself and to God that I would find a way to get His story out. Not long after that happened, I received an e-mail from a man by the name of Robert Morast saying that he wanted to write a book about LifeLight. I hadn't communicated with Robert in years, probably since he had moved away from Sioux Falls years before. But God had already been preparing me to work with Robert, even though this partnership would be an odd one.

Robert is a talented journalist, but he's a man, who in my mind, is about as opposite from me as one could be. Yet, God was speaking, and I knew I should listen. I remember the first time I had met Robert. He was a young reporter and journalist at the local newspaper. I had been intrigued and drawn to his columns because of their honest and sometimes satirical approach; yet, I was a bit skeptical of reporters in general, maybe due in part to my sphere of influence from the evangelical Christian community, which many times paints the media with a broad brush as an agenda driven liberal group. But as I met with Robert, I grew to respect him and found his writing both objective and fair. He always looked for and asked the right questions before putting a story together. I am entirely grateful for his partnership in editing this story, and I count him as a friend. From concept to reality, God has used him greatly for this book.

To give fair warning, this book might convict you, as it has me. Even in writing and remembering the stories of God's faithfulness, I have felt my heart stirred again to do God's work. But I also hope this book encourages you. You see, there has never been a better time than now to reach out to a hurting world around us. As you read, I challenge you to search your own heart and ask God how you could do more with your faith on this journey called life. I promise that He will give you some good ideas. He did for me.

Acknowledgements

A Special Thank You…

Thank you to my Lord and Savior Jesus Christ who rescued me from darkness into His light, from religion to relationship, and adopted me as a child of God.

To Vicki, my lovely partner, friend, and wife who has been at my side for 38 years and who also helped write this book. This is our story, and it has brought back the memories of a lifetime. You are my love and inspiration.

To my three wonderful daughters: B.J., for the initial and creative edits on this book, for your artistic flare, and for urging me to keep writing and moving me onward to completion. Sarah, for being my date-checker, continual prayer warrior, and never-ending supporter. Rachelle, for the thoughtful editing, support, and constant encouragement.

To Zak and Josh, we couldn't ask for more Godly sons-in-laws. You are both wonderful husbands to our daughters and great fathers to our beautiful grandchildren.

To my in-laws, Dean and Nola, for the hundreds of miles you drove, on the festival grounds and off, and for always being our biggest supporters.

To my Dad and Brenda, for your support and always making sure we had an extra roof over our heads backstage.

To our dedicated staff at LifeLight, you challenge and inspire us daily. Carol and Laurelle, thank you for your extra time and effort to edit and organize the details of this book.

To our supportive Board members, you have believed in the mission and lifted our arms.

To many special friends who have stood beside us over the years.

To the Luis Palau Association and Next Generation Alliance for your support and encouragement.

To the many Pastors and their congregations who understood the value of unity and taking the Church outside the walls.

To the hundreds and hundreds of volunteers, the festival and other ministry areas could not have happened without your perseverance and hard work.

It's nearly impossible to name everyone who has been an important part of this journey! Thank you to all who have supported us and the ministry through your gifts of time, generous finances, and, most importantly, prayer.

And for this book, thank you to Robert Morast for your editing work. Your journalistic abilities and unique perspective on this project are greatly appreciated. And thank you, Anneli, for the book cover design.

To God be the Glory!

LifeLight

TAKING THE CHURCH
OUTSIDE THE WALLS

1

Taking the Church Outside the Walls

Many people reach into memories of the 1990s and pull out images of plaid flannel shirts, reflective AOL dial-up discs, or Furbies. For me, the '90s draw out scenes of sitting in church meetings.

Whether or not you're a regular church-goer, you can imagine what these meetings were like. We discussed typical church business from Sunday school materials to vacation Bible school programs, to music, to money issues, to the color of the carpet. Many of these meetings were important, which is a nice way of saying some of them weren't. Even during those important gatherings, I'd often find my mind wandering away from proposals for various church activities or theological issues that needed to be addressed. Sitting in a church, listening to people talk about church issues, I'd wander outside the moment and focus on a question that was rarely asked in those meetings: What about the people who aren't coming to church?

This question has plagued me for years, and I've long felt a burden for the scores of people who go un-churched—as many as 73 percent, depending on which survey you study. Regular church-goers often ignore such statistics because they don't think about the world outside their church. They're inside the walls of their salvation, their conduit to heaven, and since most Christians hang out with mostly Christians, they develop a type of bubble mentality where they only see, talk, and think about a life concerning Christians and Christian issues. It's hard for some of them to even entertain the idea of a life without Jesus.

Me, I've thought about that possibility all too much.

Next time you're driving to a Sunday morning church service try this: take notice of all the people who aren't going to church. Notice all the people who are tending to their lawns, washing their cars, or getting their homes ready for the big game.

Those suggestions send some Christians into rote contemplation about the level of spiritual apathy among the un-churched. Personally, I start wondering what the church is doing wrong when people feel better about staying home on Sundays rather than joining the communion of worship.

How do we reach people with the love of Christ if they are not coming inside the walls of our buildings?

What are their needs as a family or what is motivating them in their lives? Where do they get some stress relief? How did church become irrelevant to them? Is our culture's longstanding belief in God and church attendance more traditional and cultural rather than a spiritual reaction from our hearts? And, most importantly, how do we reach people with the love of Christ if they are not coming inside the walls of our buildings?

These are the questions that filled my mind during those meetings with church leaders.

In many ways, I'm still trying to find the answers to these questions. Sure, many of the faithful will counter with the one word answer—"Jesus." But the riddle here isn't who can save people, it's how we, the followers of Jesus, can bring the answer of eternal salvation to the people who need Him the most, the people who have lost contact with Jesus—or have never had that contact.

▪ ▪ ▪

I like to think I've had a long relationship with Jesus.

It started while I grew up in a little Southern Baptist church in Shelby, North Carolina, just 40 miles west of Charlotte. It was a church stooped in tradition, serving its message to a congregation of mixed ages of white southern middle-class people trying to live as they felt God instructed them to. I had a special emotional experience there as a teen when I was baptized in the church and felt I was publicly proclaiming and agreeing to the claims of Christ. I had said a prayer and sincerely asked Jesus to be my Savior. It was spiritual, emotional, and something that's stayed with me ever since.

I believe God has been walking with me, guiding me through my adult life as I try to spread His message. But, for so long, I had this mentality that being a Christian was just about what you believed, which, of course, is important. After all, Jesus said some pretty radical things.

Jesus said He and the Father, our God, are one. He said He could forgive sin. He said we could be set free and made right with God through a relationship with Him, not by a religious system of the law. Like I said, pretty radical.

To a kid still trying to figure out algebraic equations, some of these concepts were too abstract to understand without the shorthand of "just believe and you'll be fine."

You see, I did not realize until much later that finding faith was also about experiencing Jesus in a real way, the way He experienced the life around Him while He walked this earth in human form.

Think of it like this, the Bible doesn't collect stories about Jesus and His followers sitting inside buildings talking about salvation with people who understood the Gospel. They spread His will and message to the people who had not heard it. They spent time with folks in unfortunate predicaments bringing hope through the Gospel. And they weren't afraid of mingling with society's forgotten: lepers, prostitutes, and the poor. Jesus' followers weren't confined to the interior of a church or a synagogue and the comfort of protected solitude they provided.

Funny how things can change.

And I was part of the problem.

It wasn't until I was a young newlywed and had been confronted with my own sin that I began a personal walk with Jesus, growing in Him by prayer and reading the Bible for myself. At that time I realized His word was supposed to be delivered and practiced outside the walls of the church by those that called themselves Christians, not just huddled on the inside playing church with members of the choir.

There's a stereotype among some non-believers that people attend church because their family has always done so or because it's just what society tells some of us do.

The thing is, that belief isn't wrong.

Whether Christians want to admit it or not, there are some of us who view church as a way to please God by keeping score on how good we might be, or how we appear in His eyes and the eyes of others by keeping up our Sunday attendance. But, the truth is, in the end none of that matters—not how good we might think we are, what others think of us, or even how many times we've been to church—none of it. Rather, what matters is what we do with the fact that God desires a relationship with us. Our life is His creation and He is much bigger than a religious system of rules mostly set up by the schemes of man.

I suspect there are many, both within and outside the church, who view it as a place with little relevance to their daily lives. I also know there are many pastors who are praying and pleading with their members to get in the game and join Jesus on the journey outside the church walls, but that message is sometimes lost.

The topic reminds me of a trip to Vermont my family took some years ago. During the vacation my wife insisted we tour an ice cream factory because she said it would be a learning experience. You see, as a homeschool mom, she turned everything into a learning experience, even family vacations. Our three teenage daughters and I all rolled our eyes at the prospect of being led through an ice cream factory, but we begrudgingly went along. As we worked our way through the plant, I lost interest in how "this and that is made" and the little bits of the company's history that were shared with us. My attention was lost until we reached the end, the part of the tour we were all waiting for, the ice cream samples.

Now we're talking.

Keep that story in mind and imagine this: you are on a tour of an ice cream factory, not just any ice cream factory, this stuff is to die for. In fact, it's the best you've ever had. The stuff makes waiting through the tour difficult because the smell of dark chocolate swirl, vanilla bean, and fresh cream is driving you crazy with hunger and anticipation. When you finally come to the end and everyone receives free samples you ask, "How do I get more of this? I want to share it with my friends!"

The tour guide's indifferent, monotonous tone takes you by surprise.

"You can't get this anywhere outside the factory. All of the staff, all of the resources, all of the equipment is used strictly to take care of the factory and people within the facility itself. Sometimes people seek us out and wander through the doors for a tour. We give them samples, but there is no shipping department or store here. And we don't sell to retail public."

What? Are they crazy? What kind of outfit is this? How do they manage to stay in business? Can serving their employees be their purpose?

Now back to the real world, that's how many feel when they enter a church building and experience the love of Christ and the truth of His word, but then discover the dulling reality that everything given to that church is used solely to operate that church, not to reach outside the walls with real and relevant ministry. In fact, some people who step outside of the church in the hopes of growing deeper in their faith by sharing their testimony or relationship with Jesus are told that if they really want to go deeper with the Lord, they should be in the church more. Hey, church is good for its congregation on so many levels. But when we spend so much time inside the church walls at potlucks, fellowship time, Bible studies, social gatherings, Tuesday ladies' groups, Wednesday family nights, Thursday prayer nights, Friday movie nights, Saturday softball and, of course, Sunday worship services, there isn't much time left to reach outside the walls.

Stop into any random church in America and ask if they have an evangelist or local missionary. You'll find, in most cases, there are no evangelists on staff, or missionaries. Oh, there may be some special people or organizations that are supported by the church—like perhaps a food bank or foreign denominational missionaries. But, too often the average person is not encouraged to share the Good News of Christ outside the church walls in his or her own city and region.

This must change for the world to be transformed into His image.

We have a lot more than ice cream to offer. If we really believe the words of Jesus, not only about who He is but also what He says about His followers taking part in transforming the world through His power, we should be looking for every opportunity to shout it from the rooftops with passion.

We have the greatest news in all of creation, which transcends all of time. God is with us. Jesus has saved us. We dare not keep a message this important inside the walls of the church.

That's where LifeLight comes into the story.

Through the years this has been the mission of LifeLight: to breach the confines of the buildings of worship and carry the message to the masses—wherever they are.

Jesus said, "I will build my Church and the gates of hell will not prevail against it." (Matthew 16:18)

The church Jesus referred to is you and me.

He also said, "For where two or three are gathered in my name, there am I among them." (Matthew 18:20)

How about 100,000 people gathered in His glory?

That is the heart of LifeLight. Our ministry has grown from an idea sparked at a B.J. Thomas concert to a year-round ministry fueled by hundreds of supporters and sponsors who come together for the main event that attracts more than 300,000 people. It is a free Christian music festival held annually on Labor Day weekend just outside of Sioux Falls, South Dakota. At the festival we see people unified in a service without walls; where the pulpit is a stage—actually, several stages. In this Church service, the worship songs are contemporary expressions of faith by musicians who vary from rockers to Gospel singers. And the pews, well, lawn chairs and blankets make due where the church "building" is a farm surrounded by fields of alfalfa. There are no dividers. No boundaries. It's a free-flowing communion of Christ between people who attend church every week and those who haven't been there in years. And it's working.

Christians spend so much time inside church buildings that the practice trains us to become comfortable caged within a box.

But that wasn't Jesus' idea. The original Greek word for church, ekklesia, comes from two words: ek, meaning "out of" or "out from," and kaléō, meaning "I call." Church quite literally means "to those called out" and "those assembled together." Notice it doesn't say you have to commune in a building.

In fact, you and every other believer in your city constitute the Church in that community, even when you are not assembled. But we cannot receive the benefits and blessings of church until we come together. And we can't share with the un-churched when they clearly have no interest in stepping into one. That is why our LifeLight festivals have been so exciting—they bridge the people who worship out of habit and those who have rarely, or never, done so.

Church quite literally means "to those called out" and "those assembled together."

But, before we get into stories about the festival, we need to clear your mind of any stereotypes associated with the term "music festival." Put those two words together and you'll probably find your mind running through a string of associated suggestions like irreverent rock 'n' roll, drug use, sex, violence or general debauchery.

I'm not saying those things don't happen at some music festivals. But I'm fairly certain they don't mark the LifeLight experience.

For us the festival has been centered on the positive message and emotional output of bands that spread His word through music with messages that speak to the heart. Some are young rock bands and others are traditional Gospel acts. The festival is also a place where anybody can gather and share testimonials of redemption or even repent of sins without the fear of being judged or persecuted. Many people simply go to hear some music, without worrying about any aspect of religious affiliation.

And because we keep the event free of an admission charge, there's a spot for everyone regardless of age, religious background, or cultural upbringing.

This is God's design for the Church. When this happens there is such a sense of God's presence because Jesus is there in Spirit and His people are gathered in His name. The Church is gathered.

God created us to glorify Him and to worship Him, but He also gave us a mission, an assignment: to reach the world with the Gospel, the Good News of salvation. This is simply what we do at LifeLight. It really has changed lives—from kids who commit to Jesus at the prompt of a rock singer's testimony to grandmas who marvel at all the kids praying in public. Through LifeLight God has reached people beyond what we could have dreamed or imagined.

We will worship God forever, but we won't be telling people about Him in Heaven. We only get that opportunity here on earth.

As the Christian rock band, Switchfoot, says in their song "Afterlife,"

'Cause every day, the world is made.
A chance to change, but I feel the same.
And I wonder why would I wait 'til I die to come alive?
I'm ready now; I'm not waiting for the afterlife.

It seems so simple, and, thankfully, it is. It's not about religion and the habitual paces that come with worship, but a relationship with a God who loves you. I hope you have taken the simple step to call out to Him and be a follower of Christ. When you do the Bible will take on a whole new meaning as His follower, rather than as an outside observer. You are part of the Church once you have surrendered to Him. After that life will be an exciting journey. In spite of the trials and troubles you may encounter, God will be with you.

In light of all of this, it becomes clear that we cannot just go to church, we cannot just do church, but we must become the Church if we are to continue being obedient to God.

2

Divine Hand

For many well-meaning people, Christian or otherwise, revisions often creep into the retellings of their past, their personal history. Some people use this method as a tactic to increase the drama as the events in their life unfold—like the common "rags to riches" motif that is thread so tightly throughout our culture. Others rewrite their own history in order to enhance their position or ignore past points of shame.

I can't do that. While I'd like to tell you I've always felt the calling to spread the message of Christ far outside the confines of the church's manmade walls, it simply wouldn't be true.

Growing up I always felt I was part of the Christian community. I called myself a Christian for years before I really understood the word and began fighting the dogmatic habits that can dull our lives with the Lord. As a child I went to church, Sunday school, and Bible camps. Somewhere during my teen years I resolved that I was going to be a successful person, an achiever who lived by a moral code. Yet, despite my ambitions, I was missing the intimate walk with God referenced in scripture.

For a time I wondered if it was real, people's path with Christ. That thought pattern led me to pride and self-righteousness. I later learned that it is through humility and an admission of my own personal need and struggles that God reveals Himself.

But it seemed like, through the years, God sent me occasional messages to remind me that I was part of a plan that ran counter to convention. Sometimes His instruction came via a voice or an impulse. Other times, the lesson was less obvious in its delivery, but still as impactful.

Like during a trip in 1978 when Vicki and I were driving south on I-29 through South Dakota for a vacation in California. We were young. We'd been married for two years, but still weren't even old enough to drink legally. We happily cruised down the road in our little Nissan hatchback that was packed tight with a tent, sleeping bags, and some food. We talked about our careers and dreams for the future. I was working for my father-in-law and had great aspirations of assisting in the family business. Vicki was dreaming of babies and what our life would look like with children. It was our first real vacation as a couple, and we were blissfully excited as we traveled westward.

There was no time to react or panic. It was going to hit us head-on.

Without warning and seemingly out of nowhere, a white pickup truck was speeding toward us, driving down the wrong side of the interstate. There was no time to react or panic. It was going to hit us head-on.

And next thing I know, I was looking in my side mirror and

seeing the truck barreling down the freeway beyond us. The truck was about to crash into us one second, and then it was behind us the next. Just like that.

To this day I'm not quite sure how it missed us, but in a split second the vehicle was behind us still driving the wrong direction, as if it had passed right through us or as if someone had picked the truck up and guided it over us.

We pulled over to the side of the road and marveled in disbelief as to what had just happened. Looking back now, it's still quite difficult to explain. But I do know this, I don't remember calling on God to save us or even having time to say anything.

Sitting there in our over-packed Nissan, Vicki and I looked at each other and said, "Wow, thank you God."

Clearly God was telling us, "It is not your time yet; I have things for you to do."

There wasn't a voice or a flashing neon sign, but there was the lesson—just minutes after we were planning our future, God executed one of those unexplainable moments in life that reminds us we are not in control. He is the guiding hand.

Again, fighting the temptation to revise my history, I can't say that the idea for LifeLight or my commitment to the idea of church outside the walls was born just after that truck somehow avoided crashing into us. But, that moment reminded me that I needed to follow a higher plan. I've been listening, watching, and trying to understand it ever since.

■ ■ ■

Whether through miraculous traffic movements or minor motions of natural delight, God is speaking to people and intervening in lives all over the world every day.

It is easy to pawn things off on coincidence, and it can seem impossible that there is a divine hand of God responding to our prayers—and sometimes working even with the lack of them. He's there, shepherding us through life every step of our journey. He's there, even if He does not always choose to intervene in spectacular ways.

Skeptics, or even people blessed with the objective ability to consider all aspects of a given situation, might call these stories like our traffic miracle nothing more than fortunate circumstances explained by fact. But there are so many stories similar to ours from so many places around the world that it's difficult to deny the idea that someone greater than ourselves is guiding us toward a higher purpose.

These stories happen to regular people every day. It's up to us to find the significance of our part in this plan.

That reminds me of a young Haitian man named Zachary who we met during a mission trip to his country. During the trip my son-in-law, Josh, was sharing the story about how he came to faith with a group of young people. For much of his childhood Josh had to raise himself. His mom had left the home and his father was involved with alcohol and drugs. At times Josh lived with different people and by age 14 he was sometimes trying to survive on the streets. By 15 he had been convicted of 30 counts of grand theft auto and was sentenced to juvenile prison. While on trial a local pastor pleaded on his behalf for leniency and Josh was placed on house arrest—where he could only go to school, work or church. So, Josh went to church and the pastor explained to Josh how the love of Christ was flowing through him and the people of the church. This same love began flowing through Josh once he committed his life to Christ. His life has since been transformed in a positive way and he's felt a call to share his story with others.

Considering the oppression and broken spirits that were

found in Haiti, Josh seemed the perfect person to share his story to the Haitians. He talked about how God had forgiven him and made him clean and how He could do the same for everyone. Josh and Rachelle, his wife and my daughter, even discussed how people can remain sexually pure until marriage.

The testimony was captivating, but as Josh finished a tall Haitian man named Zachary raised his hand and said, "I want to know what the purpose of this meeting was." That's not exactly what you want to hear after sharing your life story as a conduit to the Gospel of Christ. Josh recapped that Jesus could change lives as it says in the scripture. I'll never forget Zachary's words that followed, "Last night, I knelt by my bed, lit a candle and prayed, 'God, if you are real please reveal yourself to me.' Then, this morning I got up and started walking down the road and an invisible hand drew me to this place on top of the mountain." Zachary said as he was walking his girlfriend texted him, asking where he was, and telling him to come over for sex, but he just ignored it and kept walking as this "hand" led him to this place up on the hillside. "I don't want to just pray a prayer and have everything be the same like I have seen so many people do," he said. "I want real change like I have heard you talk about."

"This morning I got up and started walking down the road and an invisible hand drew me to this place on top of the mountain."

Zachary gave his whole heart to the Lord that day. Later, his girlfriend did the same. They've since been married. Zachary has attended Bible school in Haiti and been involved in the operation of a youth ministry at the foot of the hill where he met Jesus. He says he wants to start a church, but not an ordinary church, one that is focused on people who are broken, and the people outside the walls.

Perhaps some of you feel you were drawn to a particular place or event to hear clearly from God about His plan and purpose for you. In the Bible, Jeremiah 29:11 says, "'For I know the plans I have for you,' declares the LORD, 'plans for welfare and not for evil, to give you a future and a hope.'"

Isn't it great that God cares about us and knows our future?

3

God Speaks

It's been said, "If you want to make God laugh, tell him your plans."

Well, I've never heard God laugh, but I'm pretty sure He's chuckled at my plans many times through the years. But it wasn't until 1997 that I realized how true that saying can be.

As I looked back at the story of my life in doing the research for this book, 1997 stood out as the year when everything changed for my family, our faith, and the ministry.

At the time, my family and I were living the "good life" in Sioux Falls on a small acreage right outside of town. The carpet cleaning and restoration business Vicki and I had started in 1989 was doing well and providing a fairly fine livelihood for ourselves and our three daughters who were 11, 10 and 9 years old at the time. They were enjoying blissful childhood turning our tree house into their command central as they tooled around our

5-plus acres on an old golf cart and cared for our menagerie of animals. We were comfortable, we had everything we "needed," our lifestyle was simple, not extravagant, and our girls had been provided for and did not know want.

We felt God had blessed us, and by societal standards, we were successful. Yet Vicki and I had an uneasy feeling. We felt as if there was more for us in our spiritual lives, but we couldn't put our fingers on the issue or grasp what was causing this sensation, even after praying about it.

We had surrendered our lives to Him shortly after we were married and had served in many areas out of passionate obedience—things like promoting Christian concerts, heading up the local Mothers of Preschoolers (MOPS) group, joining the Christian Business Men's Committee, serving in our church, working with refugees, providing foster care, and even ministering to those in prison. We wondered what had happened to the life of faith we used to have? What happened to the radical movement of God we had once known in our earlier life? We had been faithful, obedient Christians. As it turned out, God had plans for us to reconnect with our past and satisfy those longings rumbling inside us.

We regularly went to a Christian music festival in the '90s, bringing along our young children each year and experiencing how God could reach teens through the music and the message presented while thousands of Christians gathered to lift up the name of Jesus. We could plainly sense the presence of God. We would sit and talk with like-minded friends about having something like it in our hometown.

Then, in 1997, a Christian-themed festival came to Sioux Falls, the Franklin Graham Festival to be exact. I greatly admired Franklin Graham, the son of modern America's most well-known evangelical figure, Billy Graham. In case you've lived under a rock for the past 50-some years, Billy Graham counseled presidents and spread the Christian message to millions of people through his televised specials and traveling crusades that blended testimony and music as a presentation of Christ.

Franklin continued his father's legacy as a man dedicated to preaching the word of God throughout the world. While his father's crusades were more traditional, Franklin's festivals merged the words of the Bible with performances by artists who were a little more hip for the younger generation. He also moved his festivals outdoors to be in the open instead of closed off like stadium crusades.

I remember hearing the news of the festival and thinking, "Wow! This is great. How awesome to see people and churches come together around the unity found in Jesus!"—and it was. Franklin preached from the Bible and contemporary Christian music stars Michael W. Smith and the Newsboys provided a penetrating soundtrack that resonated with the faith of the people. Because the Gospel of Jesus was presented in a relevant and contemporary fashion, the crowd responded in a way that was different than inside a church. You could see the emotions and religious barriers of various people breaking down as many went forward to confess their sins or receive prayer for a spiritual need, hurt, or deep loss.

More than 30,000 people filled the county fairgrounds for that festival, which was quite a feat considering that Sioux Falls, as South Dakota's largest city, only had a population of about 140,000 at the time. It was inspiring. It was encouraging. It was challenging. It was awesome as the sounds of contemporary music sent a chorus of praises heavenward.

Afterward, I remember a local radio talk show host speaking about how the marketing of the festival must have been really good for that many people to show up. I thought, "It wasn't clever marketing that made this event a success." To quote a

Newsboys' song, "It's a spirit thing" that brought all those people together.

The unity the local churches had found that day under Franklin Graham's banner was inspiring, but it lasted for only a short season and then faded like a fog.

The impact on me didn't fade, however. A feeling hovered over us for months after the Graham festival; it was a strong pull, a sense really, that the festival crowd of believers, new and old, young and elderly, traditional or nondenominational is how the Church is meant to be.

■ ■ ■

That fall, not long after the Graham festival, I was sitting inside the Metrodome stadium that was home to the NFL's Minnesota Vikings and the MLB's Minnesota Twins with thousands of men and boys gathered for a Promise Keepers event. The place was packed and a band had just finished leading us all in singing. The feeling of joining 50,000 or more other men in seeking communion, encouragement, and peace with each other and God was overwhelming and incredible. We sat together listening to testimonies from many motivational speakers who challenged us in our faith in ways that, at times, felt like a locker room pre-game pep talk.

> But this voice was different, and so was its direction.

Perhaps not so coincidentally, the evangelical men's organization was founded by former University of Colorado football coach Bill McCartney. His organization took on an excitement and passion modeled after his days as "Coach McCartney."

Tears had just been welling up in my eyes from the emotion

of the music. It was powerful. I settled into my seat and began to listen to the talks and then I heard a voice.

Now, this isn't unusual at a Promise Keepers event as there's often a man speaking to the mass of men about being committed to God, our family, and each other.

But this voice was different, and so was its direction.

"Take your family on a mission's trip to Mexico."

At first I didn't really know where the thought came from. The thought was not in my brain one second, and the next I'm thinking about Mexico.

I was tempted to turn to see if the guy sitting next to me was trying to tell me what to do.

He wasn't.

I focused back on the stage to make sure I wasn't misunderstanding the message.

I wasn't.

It had to be God.

My only thought was, "What?!"

Now, some of you might be thinking, "If God spoke to me, I'd drop to my knees and swear my devotion to Him and anything he told me to do!"

It doesn't work like that.

The sound wasn't audible, just a voice inside my head. Some call it that still, small voice—one we only hear when we are quiet and slow our lives down long enough to listen. It can be a thought He gives you, or a feeling. It can even be something you read. I've found whatever the delivery method, it's best to listen and take heed.

But, Mexico? With my whole family?

I had never been to Mexico and do not recall one speaker at the conference mentioning anything about family missions. Even as I searched for all logical and explainable reasons why I'd be thinking about taking my family on a mission trip to Mexico, I knew the voice was from God

After returning home I shared what I'd heard with my wife. I looked her straight in the eyes and told her I wanted to take our 9, 10, and 11 year old daughters into Mexico on a short-term mission trip.

Her immediate response? "Let's go!"

Vicki is much more spontaneous than me. She is a master at multi-tasking and multi-thinking. She's also game for most anything, but I was surprised at her response on this one.

We had talked about taking our kids to Disney World that same year, but we knew that we wouldn't be able to afford both a vacation and a mission trip, so we did the parental unthinkable and let our daughters decide. We asked them, "Do you want to go to Disney World or spend 10 days on a cramped bus and in a poverty-stricken desert?"

The three of them lined up and hardly looked at each other before unanimously chiming, "Mexico."

I was blown away by their response. To this day, thinking about it still makes me very proud.

As she often does, Vicki began to take charge right away and put things into motion finding a way to get to Mexico. After researching a number of organizations, we couldn't find many who focused on taking families on mission trips, though there were plenty that specialized in excursions for teens or adults.

After coming up short on our search, we finally discovered International Family Missions from Lafayette, Colorado, which specialized in mission trips combining individual families into a large group of about 20 to 40 for 10 days.

In the early planning stages IFM's founder, Kathy Hart, asked Vicki how large our group was.

"A group? ... I don't have one. But I'll get one."

The trip was in four months, and we would need to commit to it soon or IFM would offer the slot to another group.

So Vicki got creative. She pulled out her Christmas card list, and started making calls.

She'd lead with, "Hey, we are taking our family on a mission trip to Mexico in February ... want to go with us?"

I've always thought that the simple fact that they were not only asked, but asked by my passionate wife, was important to those friends. Vicki's contagious spirit was infectious, and she was enthusiastically committed to Mexico. Many people said they would have to think about it or pray about it, which was understandable. But I was surprised at how many of our Christmas card friends instantly said, "Count us and our family in." Soon, we had found our group of 40 people. It came together so quickly it seemed as though God was putting the group together Himself. Frankly, I was humbled by it all after my initial lack of faith in responding to the call to take my family to Mexico.

As I look back on this missions trip, I see that it was a life changer for me. At the time, I was enthusiastic about going but didn't understand how prideful passion can get in the way. God was about to deal with me on this trip to change my outlook for the future in a more deliberate way than He had done to me in the past. His divine hand was gently upon me.

■ ■ ■

That bus to Juarez, Mexico, forever changed our lives, and that of our children.

There we were going to a foreign country with no knowledge of what lied ahead of us. We were anxious, excited, and a little apprehensive about what would await us beyond the border of El Paso, Texas. But here we were a group of people from different denominations, and of different ages, all acting as representations of the body of Christ and each had their own expectations.

We knew what we were doing what was right; we were acting as the church was meant to be—outside the walls of a building.

We had wonderful guidance from the people at IFM. They didn't just talk about what to expect on the trip; they expressed a contagious passion for the oppressed people of Mexico. Their experiential wisdom was quite helpful as well, especially their lessons about taking the low road as opposed to the high road. As the Bible says in Philippians 1, "Esteem others higher than yourself, and in lowliness and meekness minister to others." Through their example, we learned how to respect the culture of the people we would be ministering to as opposed to assuming our ways are absolute and correct.

Still, as we crossed the border into this city that's become one of the most dangerous in North America, we didn't know what to expect. Most of us had never been on an international mission trip and we weren't prepared for the significant culture differences and economic disparities we saw. Thousands upon thousands of people were living in cardboard boxes and cheap pallet homes built from materials that looked like what we would throw into the garbage. I had seen poverty and homelessness before, but this was way beyond my expectations and, even worse, appeared to be the norm for a lot of Mexican people.

But they weren't the only ones with needs; I needed to have my pride broken by God.

We had been warned about the conditions, but none of us could grasp the reality of them until we saw the scene firsthand.

Without a safety net like social agencies to help improve their lives, these people had needs that were far beyond what we had seen in the U.S.

But they weren't the only ones with needs; I needed to have my pride broken by God.

Before we arrived in Mexico, I thought we would be crossing the border to help these poor Mexicans find salvation by spreading the Gospel and then all their problems would be fixed. Simple, right? When I witnessed the poverty, I couldn't wrap my mind around the sheer size of it all. One look around could cause you to become hopeless with the realization that you could never build enough homes, pass out enough rice, or heal enough hurts to help them all.

Suddenly, my pride had been replaced with doubt. Could we, this group of 40 people on their first mission, really make a difference? Yes, but we had to become true missionaries sharing the glory of God rather than a group of compassionate tourists expanding our resumes of good deeds via another interaction with the unfortunate. We had to focus on the one or few that God had put in front of us.

As we visited these peoples' homes our children played with their children. We shared meals together, visited widows and orphanages, and made crafts together. We sang together, worshipped together, and blew up animal balloons in the streets while sharing the Good News that Jesus Christ loved them. As we helped cook and serve food for the families in a rundown feeding center, the joy we received was like no other. It all felt right, yet it was measured with a sense of brokenness we hadn't felt before. God was working in our hearts, stripping away pride, and showing us the world that He loved so much. He showed us the world through His eyes.

Each day ended with a prayer gathering involving our Mexican brothers and sisters. Their prayers were so genuine and passionate, coming straight from their hearts. My heart was deeply stirred each time they prayed.

"Thank you God for supplying all my needs," they would pray, even when it seemed to me that they had nothing. "Thank you for sending the Americans to us, God, we pray for them."

I soon realized we weren't there helping their spiritual needs; they were helping ours.

It broke me. As I thought back to sitting in that chair at the Promise Keepers gathering, I realized God wasn't only sending me to Mexico so I could spread His message and heal the souls of these Mexicans; He sent me there to repair my own spiritual health.

I was humbled to see how men, women, and children would gather for a Bible club presentation in a poor neighborhood to sit, watch, and lean on every word.

I had said I wanted to share the Good News of Christ, so I was challenged in that first little gathering. Two young men, who didn't look too engaged or too friendly, were sitting on the tin roof of a small, nearby shack. Joe Hart, our IFM leader said to me, "I thought you wanted to share the story of Jesus with people? Go up there, sit with those guys, and tell them about Jesus." So I stood on a chair and then looked to the guys to help me shimmy up to the tin roof of the shaky pallet board home. My nerves were screaming, "What if this shabby tin roof falls through?! What if they push me off?!"

Well they didn't push me off, and I sat down beside them, offered some crackers and a PB&J sandwich from my backpack and tried to communicate with them through some broken Spanish, but mostly English. Fortunately, one of them could speak a little English.

After we watched the children's skit, I prayed with them and handed them each a Spanish New Testament, which they gladly accepted. I'm not sure what their fate is or what they did after

I struggled to get down from that roof. But, as I stepped back down from the little house, I looked at our team all at work — some working with children on crafts, some praying with women, some in a pickup soccer game with the teens, it made me smile to see God was at work through His body, the Church, as we were stepping out in faith outside the walls of a building.

> He sent me there to repair my own spiritual health.

As our group debriefed during the long bus ride home one thing Joe said was, "Don't make hasty decisions after this trip. Spend some time praying and thinking before you make life changes." He likened the trip to the famous C.S. Lewis novel The Chronicles of Narnia. We had been through the wardrobe door and were coming back through to a world we could never see the same way again. And Joe was right; we couldn't return to "business as usual" when we returned home.

We struggled with how to come to terms with what we had seen. Life in the U.S. looked different to us after the Mexico excursion. Our standard, middle-class home now looked like one of affluence. I remember our first day back at home, and the girls said we were out of milk. Vicki burst into tears at the realization that we had everything we needed at our fingertips—we only had to jump in the car and drive to a store. We weren't dependent upon God to provide for our needs as the Mexican believers were. In the days, weeks, and months after that trip, our family became more thankful, more reflective, and more generous to others. God gave us a heart for the needs of others. We were trading our hearts for His.

Peter Parker learned after becoming Spider-Man, with great knowledge comes great responsibility. Combine that thought with this scripture in James 1:27, "Religion that God our Father accepts as pure and faultless is this; to look after orphans and widows in their distress and to keep oneself from being polluted by the world." Our hearts were broken and convicted. We had new knowledge, and now we were responsible to the orphans and widows we just met.

Each team member on that trip to Mexico was changed as almost everyone experienced some sort of miracle or divine word from God during the experience. One revelation received by Amber, a young high school student, was so strong that a week after she returned home, her parents called me asking what happened with their daughter. It seemed she was acting different and crying since she got home; she even got rid of the TV in her bedroom. Amber had established heart-to-heart relationships in Mexico, and God got a hold of her heart, that's what happened! Amber, like us, could no longer plead ignorance about the plight of people just over our border. Nor could we plead ignorance about the lack of relevancy of the church to our culture and world issues.

Similarly, on a family level, we were torn. Should we sell our house and move to Mexico to become missionaries? The feeling of uncertainty was uncomfortable.

So we prayed on it, and waited for instruction. Then that still small voice returned, "Take the Church outside the walls, bring light into the darkness."

4

Hooked on a Feeling

"Take the Church outside the walls."

What did it mean? What did God really want us to do?

We had no clear idea.

But if the lesson of going to Mexico taught me anything, it was to listen to this message and confirm it in God's Word.

Naturally, my family and I prayed for clarity.

As we prayed and thought about the direction, the cloudy command became clearer and began to take form. God had given us the scripture years ago. He had also given Vicki and I a passion for His message through music.

And though we were coming off a life-changing experience in Juarez, one that compelled us to seriously consider moving there to set up a full-time ministry, we soon came to understand there were needs closer to home that required our attention.

We read Acts 1:8: "But you will receive power when the Holy Spirit has come upon you, and you will be my witnesses in Jerusalem and in all Judea and Samaria, and to the end of the earth."

To us, that scripture was the strategy. Start in our own community—our Jerusalem, then our region—our Judea, and nationally—our Samaria, then to the ends of the Earth.

That's how the early church grew.

The verse helped us realize that we didn't need to move to a foreign country to help people through the word of God. And, well, we as a family weren't supposed to. There were so many people to reach right in our backyard, and we needed to mobilize the Church to reach outside their walls with the Good News of Christ.

The principles of Acts 1:8 became our blueprint and the foundation that the LifeLight festival and our outreach missions ministry were built upon.

We knew we needed a structure, a place to build this vision. It didn't matter to us where, just as long as it was outside the walls.

With the luxury of history on your side, that message might not sound or feel so vague to you. But it was the '90s, a time when the mainstream identity of the church was still clearly set inside a building with an obvious design—you know it: rows of pews facing a pulpit and a cross, windows with multi-colored stained glass windows, a roof in the form of a steeple, a bell tower, and people running through the same motions, verses, songs, and actions that had been practiced in the church for decades and centuries.

Especially at that period in the Midwest, the idea of holding church in less regal locations like strip malls or vacated gas stations was still developing. The evangelical idea of worshipping in nontraditional ways and places was still being tested in a

Christian community committed to habit.

Mass media was also nearly closed off to us as a validated source of ministry. Few people in mainstream pop-culture acknowledged the large audience that buys tickets to concerts featuring Christian musicians or Christian movies. It was not considered a genre or demographic. It was just a symptom of religion.

Now I'm not trying to create an "Us vs. Them" scenario here. Rather, I'm just trying to illustrate the past's subtle differences from today and how the idea of starting a free music festival in Sioux Falls, South Dakota, was rather distinct, certainly unique, and maybe a bit anti-establishment.

Yet, it felt so right.

The thoughts of how we could make the festival and the ministry a reality took Vicki and I back to years earlier when God had reached us through music, and we had promoted Christian concerts in Sioux Falls as "LifeLight." We remembered the festivals we had been to like Sonshine in Minnesota, where thousands of people gathered in a field to worship along with the bands and seek out God through the evening message.

We recalled the Jesus movement festivals of the '70s we had watched on TV with their early Christian music pioneers such as rock bands Petra and 2nd Chapter of Acts. We thought about Larry Norman singing and rockin' to "Why Should the Devil Have All the Good Music." I remember feeling we had finally heard music in the style we enjoyed, yet the words of the music spoke life to us as Christians, instead of conflicting with our hearts.

We also thought of Keith Green—no relation, I can only wish. He was a church icon who shaped much of Christian music in the late '70s and '80s. He once said, "I repent of ever having recorded one single song and ever having performed one concert if my music, and more importantly my life—has not provoked you into Godly jealously, or to sell out more completely to Jesus!"

Talk about an inspiration!

We thought about all these spiritual forerunners and how they shaped aspects of contemporary Christianity. But we also considered how they had influenced us as individuals and as Christians.

Now, armed with God's call to send His message past the confines of church and the reflections of our personal moments of inspiration, the vision of LifeLight began to shine again, reborn as a calling of festivals, missions, and outreach.

We just had to move and encourage the establishment of churches to join us.

■ ■ ■

When Vicki and I were first married, back in the days before children, I used to enjoy singing music around the house. My repertoire consisted mostly of the top 40 list and popular silly love songs by groups like Boston or the Bee Gees.

I'm sure Vicki loved it.

I was also a huge B.J. Thomas fan. I was eagerly anticipating his concert coming to Sioux Falls, especially since the town didn't attract a lot of concerts in the late 70s, despite being the state's largest city. One day in particular, I can remember belting the lines from the B.J.'s top five 1969 hit "Hooked On a Feeling." And I sang it rather well, in my opinion. I was serenading her to buildup to the announcement that I was going to take her out on a date to Thomas' concert.

There was just one problem, as I was singing, "I'm hooked on a feeling. I'm high on believing that you're in love with me," Vicki asked me, "Who sings that?"

"B.J. Thomas," I answered with a grin.

"Well, then let him sing it."

I feigned hurt, and we had a good laugh out of it.

We did go on that date to hear Thomas sing some of his good old love songs. Then, about halfway through the set, Thomas stopped singing, looked at the audience, and said, "The rest of the concert will be from some of my Gospel albums that you can find at your local Christian book store."

He went on to share that God had changed him completely from the inside out, that he had overcome alcohol and drugs, and he was a new person who would like to sing some of his new music as testimony.

After hearing all that, Vicki and I looked at each other and said, "What's a Christian book store?"

You see, we had been raised in the church but had no real understanding of how it affected our lives outside of church. Oh, we were good people (and credit that to our upbringing), but an ongoing, daily walk with Jesus was somewhat foreign to us.

As Thomas switched to his Christian material, the songs started speaking to our souls with a sense of peace and joy that was still fun and relevant. It sounds rather cliché, but it was like God was speaking through the music in a way we could appreciate. That concert, that music, started us on a journey to look to the Bible to see what it had to say. Christian music opened our eyes to see that not only could the Bible and its message of hope, peace, and love be true, but that it pertained to our contemporary lives—something much of the music we sang in church services was not able to do for us.

I wanted more.

We began looking into other Christian music and the Biblical lessons the lyrics contained. We were not questioning the authority of the church or the Christian faith, but we began to wonder about how this faithfully presented Gospel seemed to be failing to be relevant to our peers.

Not long after that Thomas concert I saw a poster for a rock concert that was to be held at the Sioux Falls Coliseum. It was clear the featured act was not the typical rock band.

As I wandered into the venue my suspicions were confirmed. This band, 2nd Chapter of Acts, was singing ballads of worship and pop rock that were different than anything I had ever heard in church. The group was loudly proclaiming its faith and the peace and hope they had found in Christ. That night I had no clue that these rock 'n' roll siblings were early pioneers in the contemporary Christian music movement. All I cared about was that the music was good! I called my wife, who was at a Christian women's meeting and told her, "You have to get down here. This is real music!"

Later we found a Christian bookstore and discovered a wide genre of Christian music in every style. I think we bought nearly every Gospel album that B.J. Thomas had recorded, and quickly began a collection of other contemporary Christian artists. While there is nothing wrong with traditional church hymns, they rarely stuck with me after I passed from the pew into the parking lot. This music spoke the message of God to us the whole weeklong.

In those early years of discovering Christian music, we became addicted to groups like the rock band Petra, whose lyrics played an important part in planting the seeds for LifeLight.

Greg X. Volz, the original lead singer for Petra, recently said to me, "We were outside the walls of the church, having concerts in the streets if necessary." It was a necessity, as a lot of the churches would not accept Petra's music, even though the band's rock songs often carried a stronger message than I had heard in many churches.

It wasn't just a bias against Petra. In the '70s and '80s many churches were taking part in a crusade against rock music, blaming it for the corruption of their young. Even when popular secular artists admitted their Christian faith and how it influenced their work, the church failed to embrace them. It was, and at times still is, embarrassing how the churched population mistreated these musicians with didactic accusations of hedonism and, sometimes, Satanism. Even B.J. Thomas fell victim to this prejudice.

It's a trite thing to say that "music means a lot" to people. But the phrase is overused for a reason; it's true. Especially when there's faith attached to it.

About the same time Vicki and I started frequenting our local Christian bookstore we met a man named Bruce Fischer who worked in the bookstore and was a worship leader. He was also in a heavy metal Christian band named Zion. When you saw and heard the longhaired Rex, lead vocalist for the group, you knew you certainly were not listening to any "church" or praise music. I think these guys were a bit ahead of their time, but nonetheless, we started attending Zion concerts and were amazed at how the group was changing the local youth. I mean truly changing them!

Zion would play in a park or at a school and kids would come to the stage at the end of concerts to confess their sins and ask for prayer for horrific life situations. It was moving to see so many young people seeking something real from the Church. It was so moving, in fact, that one day Vicki told me she wanted to quit her job and help manage this rock band.

It made no sense. We were a young married couple depending on our two jobs to pay the bills. Could we make it on just my income as a salesman? I didn't think so. I had a plan for our lives and eventually wanted kids. Besides, we were both still fresh in our new commitment to God. But she told me she felt God had revealed this to her and put the passion in her heart to do it. Vicki assured me He could work it out if we were faithful and obedient.

I knew she was right, but I was still fearful.

And God blessed her decision in spite of my lack of faith.

Still, it wasn't an easy path to step into.

The idea of booking and promoting a heavy metal Christian band as a way to minister to youth in crisis was so counter culture to traditional Christian methods that there was resistance from the churches about the entire situation.

"How could this be of God?" some pastors and churches asked. Yet we saw the fruit of changed lives through Zion's ministry, and we continued to feel and see God at work in these concerts as un-churched, hurting people would show up and hear the Gospel.

Our passion to reach young people through Zion's music continued to grow. As we gathered with friends, we would discuss the state of the Church and how we could reach those who never bothered to step foot inside of it. Out of those gatherings with dear friends, a concert ministry was formed with three other committed couples.

We called it LifeLight, based on John 8:12, "I am the Light of the world. Whoever follows me shall not walk in darkness, but will have the light of life." And together we promoted concerts which sounded the alarm that our youth needed to know Christ.

Through the years, for various reasons ranging from the myriad complexities of life to the simple reality of increasing family obligations, we got away from LifeLight. But, as I sat there in the '90s, fresh off that life-altering trip to Mexico, and with God's instruction to "take the church outside the walls, bring light into the darkness" still echoing in my head, my mind drifted back to the days of that early LifeLight ministry.

And with the pressure of God's message waiting to be spread, we realized that part of His will was to use music to spread that Gospel.

LifeLight was reborn.

5

Miracle Through Brokenness

You might call me Type A.

I'm the kind of guy who likes schedules. I'll focus on goals with laser precision, and I have no problem strategically plotting out years of my life at a time in my head. This can be a good trait for a salesman who's trying to build a secure, dependable home base for a family. But when you're following the lead of the Lord, through instructions that no one else can hear, having a Type A mindset isn't always ideal.

Trust me.

In the early '80s, Vicki and I were learning to trust and obey God. The LifeLight ministry of promoting Christian music concerts was growing and we were also now intent on starting our family.

It wasn't easy...which is another way of saying we weren't

getting pregnant.

After years of trying we were hurting as a couple and wondering why God wasn't blessing us with a child.

As you can imagine, this unexpected development was difficult for my personality and my plan.

It is in my nature, and Vicki's, to fix the problems we encounter, to make things happen. We're both the oldest children in our own families, and there seems to be something about that birth order which results in a fierce need to be in charge. And being in charge is great, until you are not. And with this, we weren't in charge. We couldn't fix the infertility problem.

I still remember the words from the medical specialist, "It is nearly medically impossible for you both to have children." The feeling was humbling because through the sober reality of those words, I was coming to grips with the fact that this was, essentially, my fault. I had a sperm count of virtually zero.

Naturally, we turned to prayer and the Bible, where we had read that God will give you the desires of your heart.

"God! We want children! Quickly, please!" We had waited years.

We know now that those desires need to line up with God's will, not ours, and that God is perfect in His timing—always. But at the time, we persisted in our hope for children, continuing to see the specialist until he finally looked at us and said, "You should just pray. There is nothing more I can do for you."

His words were utterly discouraging. Hadn't we been praying all along?

Even though we considered ourselves to be strong in our faith, it was hard to understand what God was telling us through the statement of infertility.

Making matters worse, people close to us said things like, "You can't miss what you don't have," or, "Just learn to relax, and it will happen." We felt frustrated; it wasn't as if tension and stress were the cause of the medical problem. If that were the case we would have fixed it already!

I felt inadequate as a man and we, as a couple, were devastated.

When we decided to accept the truth of our situation and pursue a child through adoption, we were told the waiting list was so long that the process could take years.

Our spirits were broken and our home was empty.

We had been learning about God and walking in His ways; yet, despite God's instructions, I was chasing my own dreams and plans. After nearly nine years of childless marriage Vicki and I were in tears as we finally prayed a prayer of desperation and release.

"God, You tell us in Your Word that You will give us the desires of our heart, and You know we want children. So, if it is not Your will for us to have children, then please take the desire from us."

I remember looking at Vicki and seeing the pain in her eyes. I was unaccustomed to seeing this look in my wife who had been so strong and confident through the years. The sight of my wife's despair caused me to fall into my own silent grief. I wanted to give her the motherhood that she wanted more than anything. But this was one thing I couldn't fix no matter how hard I tried or how much I focused on the problem.

Funny how God tends to grant your dreams after you've given up hope of achieving them on your own.

After we made that plea to God, a certain degree of doubt crept into our hearts as to whether we really meant those words.

"Did we really just pray that? God take away the desire; Your will, not mine?"

Yes, we were at peace with the admission. Even though it still hurt, we confirmed the devotion, "We give this fully to God."

Funny how God tends to grant your dreams after you've given up hope of achieving them on your own.

■ ■ ■

Less than two weeks after asking God to strip away our desire to be parents, on a seemingly random, but totally God-ordained Monday in the middle of August, Vicki got a phone call.

The adoption agency, which still had us on its waiting list, told her one of the most life-changing and faith-affirming things we've ever heard, "We have a beautiful baby for you to pick up!"

After Vicki hung up the phone, she was so excited and stunned that she had to call the agency back to find out if we were receiving a boy or girl.

It was a little girl.

Vicki rushed to my office and told the receptionist to get me out of the meeting with my boss. When she relayed the news I immediately told my boss that I would have to leave. We went straight to tell our family the good news. Our amazing range of emotions that day was unreal—excitement, anticipation, nervousness, and everything in between. It was all so fast. We were picking up a baby, our baby, the very next day.

My wife describes our adoption experience as being pregnant today and having the baby tomorrow. Since we couldn't bring ourselves to do much baby shopping before, we scrambled to find things for our empty nursery. Friends rallied to help us, and we gathered nearly everything we needed within 24 hours. And, within a week, more friends and family had sent their well-wishes via cards, gifts, congratulations, and several baby showers. We were blessed.

I think that night was filled more with counting down the hours than counting sheep. But that moment finally came when she was placed into our arms. I had never seen a more beautiful baby. We got lost in her gorgeous blue eyes. She was ours.

We named our daughter Bethany Joy; Bethany for the city where Jesus raised Lazarus from the dead, and Joy for what she brought us.

She was (and still is) perfect for us. Even as a child, she defied all those horror stories about crying, fussy babies by sleeping through the night from the first day we got her. We took her everywhere; to meetings, shopping, church, even to the Christian concerts we were still promoting. We could tuck her car seat under the ticket table we worked, and she would sleep or smile through the whole concert. Each moment with Bethany was a treasure.

It wasn't long after receiving that life changing phone call that Vicki felt like she had the flu. She was sick during the mornings and tired at times through the day and evening. Her mom told her it sounded like she was pregnant. We laughed and said, "Well that would be a miracle!" Given our previous difficulties trying to conceive and the bleak picture the fertility specialist painted for us, we had honestly not even given a thought to the fact that she might be pregnant. But we listened to her mother's intuition and I have never driven so fast to a store as I did that day to bring a pregnancy test home to Vicki.

After two torturously slow minutes, the test read positive. We laughed, shouted, cried, and celebrated. Yes, we were going to have a baby. Yes, she was pregnant. Yes, it was unbelievable.

That December, 1986, we were blessed with another baby girl, Sarah Faith. We picked Sarah from Hebrews 11:11, the chapter on the faith of Abraham and Sarah who had waited so long for their promised son, Isaac. We brought Sarah home from the hospital on Christmas day. What a Christmas that was! Vicki, I, and our two wonderful daughters, what a gift.

There was more to come.

In spite of all God had delivered to us, we were bewildered and amazed when, 14 months after Sarah was born, Vicki gave birth to our third daughter, Rachelle Hope. We chose Rachelle after Rachel from the Bible, and Hope represented God's promise to never give up hope. There we were, young parents who had only recently believed we would be childless, and now we had a home with three beautiful girls, ages two, one, and newborn.

God had healed our medical problem and opened the flood-gates, so to speak. As I look back on what God did for my family in such a short time I realize this was all on His timetable, all part of His plan for us.

■ ■ ■

This new thing called parenthood and its dramatic entrance into our lives forced us to evaluate our suddenly busy schedules.

On top of the daily duties of raising young children we were trying to trust in God's wisdom for our lives. At the time we were involved in our church, as well as many para-church ministries. Plus, we were still busy with the LifeLight concert ministry and God's desire for us to take the church outside the walls. But kids have an uncanny way of changing priorities, especially when those priorities mean trying to keep three young children in clean diapers and out of trouble.

We assumed we would continue on and even develop the ministry as our children grew around it. But God graciously reminded us that we had prayed for children for years. It was time to enjoy them and this new chapter in our lives. So, after years of promoting concerts and meeting with others to plan how to reach a generation of young un-churched people, it became clear to us and the people around us, that it was time to move on to other things. We had been given a foundation on which to raise our children and knew that God could certainly handle the music industry without us.

I quit my job as a salesman, started a small cleaning and restoration company, and spent the next 13 years providing for Vicki and our three daughters. Those years were good years. We were enjoying our family and life was smooth sailing.

And all those years, God was ready and waiting for us to say yes to the next thing He had for us. He was speaking. I just wasn't hearing His call.

6

LifeLight Festival is Born

LifeLight was reborn.

Sunny summer Sunday afternoons in the neighborhoods of Sioux Falls and rural South Dakota play perfectly to the Midwestern stereotype.

Towns are full of peace and quiet as people settle in after attending church or sleep in late to recover from a long week. The streets are mostly empty, still enough for kids to toss a football around without worrying about a car interrupting the game. The only bit of disturbance on a lazy Sunday afternoon comes from meticulous homeowners trimming the edges of their manicured lawns.

You get the picture. It's many people's domestic dream.

And some would say I was ruining it all on this first day of September in 1998.

There I was, standing on the lawn of the Good News Reformed Church, which was tucked in one such idealistic neighborhood, watching the pop band Go Fish play on the stage constructed on the church lawn near the asphalt parking lot.

The music was upbeat and had everyone dancing and clapping along. And I wanted it to be louder. Much louder. Loud enough to compel everybody in every house in earshot to unplug from their Sunday routines, come outside, and wonder where all the noise was coming from.

I wanted them to be part of the first LifeLight music festival.

■ ■ ■

We never regretted putting our ministry on hold. God had gifted us with our beautiful children, and I was intent on enjoying every moment of the fatherhood that I had once feared I would never experience. It was, and still is, wonderful. But I'd be lying if I didn't admit that to some degree, I was ignoring God's call for me.

While I was busy being dad I still attended church business meetings. Whether at a meeting or just hearing another's calling to serve in his or her local church, I was continually reminded about and burdened for the number of people who never stepped inside a church. I often asked myself whose responsibility it was to reach them and how it would happen.

And the answer coming from deep in my heart was always the same: "Take the Church outside the walls, bring light into the darkness."

After taking 13 years to build our foundation as a family, Vicki and I began to feel it was time to commit ourselves again to LifeLight and to God's will to carry the spiritual nourishment of church outside the manmade structures.

As we pondered the possibilities of what LifeLight would be as a ministry it was hard to imagine it without music. The lyrics and sounds of our favorite bands had always impacted how Vicki and I experienced our faith. And as I thought back to the concerts we promoted prior to the arrival of our daughters, it was hard not to remember how the music drew in a young crowd of people who weren't spending their Sunday mornings in a church pew. We recalled how we'd seen young men jump from the audience to the stage and ask for repentance from the Lord during those Christian rock shows.

We knew we needed to continue that legacy, but in a more focused and penetrating experience that could provide communion for the devoted while hosting an entertainment base that would attract the outliers.

After much prayer, the vision of a Christian music festival came as clearly as the voice that spoke to me about taking my family to Mexico. I just had to figure out how to make it happen. To start by asking the church for guidance seemed like a good first step.

As I approached the church leadership, I shared the vision of a one day outdoor music festival—how it could be staged on the church's property, how we could keep it free to attract anyone with curiosity for music or for God, and how it would bring us together as a church while following Jesus' command to go and make disciples.

Then I told them what I needed: $5,000 in seed money to launch the festival. I knew that was $5,000 the church and its board hadn't budgeted for.

And, the church had more than money to lose. It was putting its image and worship philosophy on the line as this venture that was decidedly atypical of what most Midwestern Christians considered to be outreach.

Pastor Glen Blumer looked at me with questioning eyes and said, "And what if it rains? What risk do we have? Could we lose the

$5000 for this festival?"

"Yep, you could lose it all," I said. "But we need to step outside the walls in faith."

To my surprise, the members of the elder board all said yes!

And we started planning for the inaugural LifeLight festival, which would take place in mere months.

The land of Good News Reformed Church was on the west side of Sioux Falls on a hill that created a natural amphitheater. I could picture it in my mind; the stage at the bottom of the hill, people filling the hillside to witness these bands that dared to blend rock music with Christian ethics. Between envisioning something like this and actually seeing it happen came a lot of work and serious planning.

As we considered how to produce this festival and what its defining characteristics would be, there were several that felt like necessities.

It had to be a free event. Something as simple as the price of a ticket couldn't be a barrier for people to attend. Plus, the love of Christ and salvation is a free gift. As an extension of the church's glory, this festival would be offered at no charge. It had to be.

LifeLight also had to be a gathering that blended various generations and cultures. God doesn't want a segregated Church; He is looking at all people, all ages, and all races.

This couldn't be the project of just one church, synod, or branch. It had to be welcoming to all people and couldn't be viewed as the domain of one particular part of Christianity. An evangelist and my friend, Luis Palau, has said many times, "When God sees the church, He sees one Church—many Congregations."

The festival had to carry and present the message of faith in Christ for salvation. Salvation is the major purpose of the Church and the command of Christ. We could not ignore the opportunity to share with the masses the truth of salvation in recognizing their sin, turning from it, and surrendering to Christ. We knew we could only tell the lost about Jesus on this side of eternity—we felt the urgency that we must share the Gospel now!

And we would use the festival as a platform to challenge the Church to partake in missions and to truly "be the church" with causes that reach outside the walls.

Also, the music and bands we were presenting had to be of top quality. They couldn't be playing cheesy "Christian-ese" music that was prevalent at various free Christian events at that time. The Lord will use anyone with the right heart, but I believe He desires excellence as something that brings Him glory. Many times we are just too cheap within the Church to pay for a good band. Sometimes, we just have to spend the money.

But back in 1998, before a single note had been plucked, we were just hoping to get the festival off without a hitch.

I believe He called us to represent Him as ambassadors by displaying the excellence of the qualities He grants us. To honor His message our events cannot be perfect, but must be done with quality in mind. Besides, a bad band isn't going to attract the secular music fans. And that's who we wanted at LifeLight—the people who don't flock anywhere where there's a "Christian" event.

That was the LifeLight manifesto of sorts. It's a set of principles that exist to this day as the festival has evolved into a 3-day affair attracting hundreds of thousands of people.

But back in 1998, before a single note had been plucked, we were just hoping to get the festival off without a hitch.

We were going to dream big even if we started small. And, believe me, we started small.

Hundreds of people from our church and the community,

young and old alike, gathered at the church. At the time seeing that crowd huddled together to hear some contemporary Christian music felt like a major victory.

In truth, it was.

As the afternoon music gave way to the message of salvation later that evening, a Free Lutheran Pastor, Michael Brandt, who was a good friend, mentor, and gifted evangelist, shared the Gospel. A small group gathered beside the stage for prayer at his invitation. This was the purpose for the whole day.

I believed that many people who were there began to grasp the concept of our festival vision. Some even compared it to the old tent revivals. Others were just curious. And many simply stood back to see if this would really catch on. We knew God had been at work that day. He still is to this day.

■ ■ ■

Two things were apparent almost immediately after the first LifeLight concluded: we would be repeating the festival 12 months later, and we needed to spread the word of God even further into the world.

Whether it was witnessing the willingness of people from different denominations to congregate in unity or the high of realizing we had pulled off an event that was ordered by God, that first festival reignited my passion to do missionary work as I realized how important it is to feed people's souls as well as their bodies. That's what true evangelism is all about.

We were soon planning another trip to Mexico with a group of families for the next year.

Sadly, the situation in Mexico had not changed much. As our bus of missionaries pulled into Juarez, I surveyed the scene and became discouraged seeing so many people in need. I knew we couldn't take care of them all.

It's a rather sour reality to realize. But, I had always remembered what was told to me by Joe Hart from International Family Missions before our first trip about how we need to make sure that while trying to give people material things to make their lives better, these physical gifts are of no value if we do not tell them the Good News of Christ. We will never have enough blankets, or enough beans and rice, or be able to build enough homes to take care of all the needs in this world. We certainly want to encourage providing for the needs of the poor, and we still do so with every mission trip, but we also want to make sure we are proclaiming the Good News of salvation as proclaimed by Jesus. I know God had been guiding our lives toward helping people understand the promise of His salvation. And I'm sure the people who joined us on that mission trip felt the same as we all experienced something that sure felt like a miracle.

Our group was leading a children's ministry in a meager metal building that, if nothing else, provided us all a reprieve from the sun's blistering rays. The young children were doing craft projects with glitter and glue, and most of them were gathered with their mothers who appeared to appreciate the break from routine by participating in some simple crafts with us.

We want to make sure we are proclaiming the Good News of salvation as proclaimed by Jesus.

After the craft session was concluded, a long line formed as we served juice, apples, and sandwiches to the families. While the people filtered through the line, a few members of our team started counting heads for an estimate of how many sandwiches we'd need to make. It soon became clear that we didn't have enough meat and bread to make sandwiches for all the people. There were just too many hungry children.

We sent some of our group to a market to search for more food. If they didn't return in time, we'd just have to tell them we ran out of food. We did all we could.

It's interesting how many times God steps in for an assist after hearing somebody earnestly say, "We did all we could."

Well, he was listening that day in Juarez, Mexico.

As we were handing out sandwiches, preparing for the last one to be given away, an amazing thing happened—we didn't run out! Every person who stepped into line left with food!

It was curious because we knew how many bagged lunches we had and the number of hungry people far exceeded that tally. Then a team member, Jolene, stated matter-of-factly what now seems like the obvious, "Look! We have enough for every last child and from a human standpoint that is not possible. Just do the math."

She was right; it shouldn't have been possible. But the line was empty, every child was seated, and each of them had a bagged lunch with a sandwich included.

"God clearly provided more food for us to feed all these kids," Jolene added.

Times like that are when we learn God is in control and will take care of everything if we just trust him. It's a simple lesson, yet we seem to need to keep learning it over and over. Fortunately for us He is faithful in spite of our wavering faith.

After we returned to South Dakota, and as we prepared for the second LifeLight festival, our faith began to dip a bit. We weren't sure how we could do the festival again because we were overwhelmed with our family business, Vicki was homeschooling, and we needed to organize a bigger, better talent lineup to keep the momentum going for another festival. I knew our faithful friends and committee were on board. Pastor Glen was certainly with us. In fact, he shared the vision for the festival, but we would need at least $10,000 as a cushion to advance with the festival that year.

The money concerns became secondary as we were struck with another trial. One we could not have ever predicted.

One day Vicki had slipped her arm around our middle daughter, Sarah, who was 12. Vicki noticed something was wrong; it felt like Sarah wasn't sitting up straight. We took her to a specialist who told us that Sarah had extreme scoliosis and would need back surgery to fuse her spine in about an 18-inch section.

This would be a very difficult surgery but with her spine having such an extreme curve at only 12 years of age she would need surgery soon to prevent further damage. Our spring and summer consisted of trips to Minneapolis and preparation for the surgery. The night before the procedure, Sarah saw the concern in Vicki's eyes and said, "Don't worry, Mom. Just trust in God. It's all OK."

Such faith.

One of the harder things I've had to do is watch them wheel my daughter into surgery and not have any control over the several hours that followed.

Thankfully, Sarah sailed through the surgery. A few days later we transported her home in a bed in the back of a van.

Maybe in part because of Sarah's love for Christian music and what it meant to our family, we moved forward with the festival plan knowing we were being obedient to God in the process.

Once again, He rewarded us as the crowd doubled for the '99 festival, which featured Christian musical acts like Sierra and Solomon's Wish. It was starting to feel more like an actual festival, not just an afternoon on a church lawn.

We asked Pastor Glen to preach at the festival that year, and as he was finishing his message he asked for people who wanted a change in their lives, who wanted to commit their lives to Jesus to come to the stage for prayer.

I was eager to see what would happen next. Others were too,

apparently, as the crowd was silent and everyone remained still while the sun melted into dusk.

It was too still. Nobody was making the move to the stage.

I was disappointed, but I began to console myself, "At least the message went out. We are not responsible for the results, that's God's job."

Then, almost on cue, a young teenage boy stood up from his place on the grass and walked to the front of the stage. After a moment his dad joined him, putting his hand on his son's shoulder. It was a moving moment, seeing father and son standing unashamed before the crowd and before God. I knew Heaven was watching too, as Jesus said in scripture, "So everyone who acknowledges me before men, I also will acknowledge before my Father who is in heaven." Matthew 10:32.

If we are faithful in presenting the message, it is God and His Spirit who will deal with people's hearts.

It's a verse worth remembering, as is the fact that we can't judge a ministry by crowd size or the number of people who publicly ask for God's salvation. If we are faithful in presenting the message, it is God and His Spirit who will deal with people's hearts. And most of the time, we won't be present to witness the results.

■ ■ ■

In 2000, we planned for the third LifeLight festival thinking about the original vision for it all—an event inspired by the scope of music and testimony we'd experienced at the Franklin Graham festival that toured through Sioux Falls years before. We wanted more national bands that could attract a larger, more diverse audience. And we wanted plenty of un-churched people to come;

we were aiming the message toward them!

The plan looked great on paper, but how would we do this? Miraculously God again provided, as He always does.

In our third year, with a growing reputation and some media support, we were hoping the festival would attract a more substantial crowd than it had in the past. So, we set another goal: if 5,000 people showed up on that church lawn, we would move future LifeLight festivals to a larger, more suitable location.

But, you can't dream bigger than God.

That year it started out cloudy and damp. Even if it didn't rain, the conditions were perfect for holding back the people who don't like to get wet.

By that afternoon, the weather had done a complete 180 degree turn. It was beautiful, and plenty of people showed up.

With a sizeable crowd, we were forced to turn up the volume on our PA system, which meant flirting with passing the established volume limits for that mostly residential neighborhood. As the LifeLight fan favorite, Go Fish, was working through their set of uplifting and inspirational songs, we were quickly closing in on the 9:30 p.m. deadline for our noise permit.

As you can imagine, a public outdoor concert on a Sunday evening in a neighborhood full of family homes isn't exactly a conspicuous thing. This is one reason why police were patrolling the event; to ensure LifeLight didn't inspire the kind of craziness or rowdy nature of some other music festivals. And, wouldn't you know it, as we were nearing the limits of our noise permit, an officer pulled his cruiser up to the grounds for an inspection. Feeling a little nervous, I approached him, expecting to be strictly reminded of the guidelines.

He relayed the report of one noise complaint.

"Officer, we'll be done in about 15 minutes," I said. "Our sound permit gave us until 9:30 to finish."

"That's OK...look at those kids by the stage," he said, referencing the mass of young people pressing toward the stage, enthusiastically enjoying their music. "This is great!"

Relief flooded through me. Once again, we knew God was up to something. Yet we also felt the potential for more, almost like there was something missing.

A pattern was developing. Each year we were doubling our crowd numbers, and that was without the lure of a huge, famous band headlining the event.

Our initial vision was to "take the church outside the walls," and we had, quite literally. But as we reflected on that third festival, we realized it would be nearly impossible to continue holding LifeLight on the lawn of the church. Part of this was physical limitations, but we had also always envisioned LifeLight as a non-denominational faith-based gathering. Holding it on the grounds of a specific church, with a specific affiliation, meant the festival would be perceived as that church's event. That meant some people just wouldn't feel comfortable attending. We wanted the "world" and community churches to feel welcome.

And to top it off, we had reached our benchmark of 5,000 people on that small church field on the western edge of Sioux Falls.

We needed another venue, and a neutral venue. We needed to do more than just take the church outside the walls; we needed to take it off the property.

7

We're Moving to the Fairgrounds

As the planning process for the 2001 festival began, we had already selected the new home we wanted for the LifeLight festival; we wanted to move it to the county fairgrounds located next to a rock quarry inside the Sioux Falls city limits. It was the same place we had seen the Franklin Graham Festival four years earlier.

The move to the fairgrounds wasn't going to be easy. Logistically it would take a higher degree of order and execution to grow the festival from an event in a suburban church's parking lot to something that conformed to a fairground setting with a concert grandstand that could hold more people than we had attracted in all the previous years of our festival combined.

The first step was convincing the fairground's manager we could do it. Fortunately for us, she had an open mind.

We explained how we had outgrown the church lawn while describing our vision and dream. She politely nodded and told us in a practical manner that local events didn't draw well in Sioux Falls and that any time an event switched locations, the audience shrunk as many of the people wouldn't migrate with it. She said we could expect 3,000 attendees at best. We said we expected more and had envisioned 10,000-plus in the future. She looked at us with a gaze of compassion, as if she understood our enthusiasm yet had reservations about how we would pull this off.

You can imagine how crazy the idea sounded to some of these faith leaders.

We talked about how we wanted them to rearrange the grandstand's layout, which basically had been a racetrack design with covered risers facing a stage with a dirt and gravel-covered general admission area between the two. We wanted them to shift the configuration by fanning out the sides to allow more people to be in the general admission section. We also wanted to add grass and provide a more amenable area around the stage.

The manager nodded, but I could see the question in her eyes, "Is this really going to happen?"

Regardless of the degree of her faith in our concept, we earned her blessing and agreed on a date, the Sunday of Labor Day weekend.

The work we needed to do to make this happen increased exponentially. But the hardest task wasn't securing people to work backstage or coordinate traffic flow patterns, it was convincing the city's various church leaders to do something many of them, and their congregants, would find challenging and possibly uncomfortable—relocating their own Sunday worship services to join our non-denominational service at the fairgrounds.

You can imagine how crazy the idea sounded to some of these faith leaders.

For one, many of them didn't know LifeLight from a flashlight. Then there's the reality that humans are creatures of habit, they like the expected nuances of a regular routine. When you tell someone that their weekly church service in the building they've sat in every Sunday for decades would be moving to a fairground for an event they don't know or care about, the reactions aren't hard to predict. Then, there's the reality that pastors and church leaders are often surrounded by or connected to people who regularly tell them how to conduct their worship services. It's not just one man or woman's will that dictates a Sunday service but a collaboration of many.

While some churches would work with similar congregations for para-ministry services or charity causes, the idea of sharing their worship services with Christians of a different denomination was (and sometimes still is) a rather uncommon thought to contemporary Christian America. Some are very liturgical in their services, others informal; some preach in the High Church format of order and ceremony while others practice Low Church principles. Some sermons are simple, others more complex.

And there I was, asking all these denominations to forgo their traditions and come together for a Sunday worship time preceding a day of concerts that some of these people might be uncomfortable with. I wanted these pastors to ignore all their routines, all the potential critics, and all their usual aids. I wanted them to come together in trust for one mission, to reach our city. I was asking them to join with me, a guy who didn't run in their religious circles, a guy whose biggest claim to the local Christian scene was staging rock concerts with a Christian message.

As you can imagine, I was a bit nervous about this portion of the LifeLight preparation plans.

To focus on casting our vision to these pastors, I took time off from my job so I could minimize distraction while setting up a series of face-to-face meetings with as many senior pastors in our city as I could convince to talk to me. I explained to each one that I believed the soul of LifeLight was about bringing the body of Christ together outside the church walls to reach the masses with the message of Jesus Christ. I told them about how our small festival in a church parking lot had grown into something that demanded moving it to the larger landscape of the fairgrounds. And, I plain and simple asked them to send their congregations to LifeLight's Sunday worship service for that one day a year.

As I summarized earlier, there's a lot of bureaucracy in the life of a church leader. But even if you have to wade through all that bureaucracy you will find at the heart of most pastors is the desire to make known the Gospel of Jesus Christ. That's the quality I appealed to as I shared my plan to bring all the Christians of Sioux Falls together for one glorious community worship service.

After hearing my heart, 12 churches agreed to relocate their service to the festival grounds and have church as one Christian body. Wow!

The first to agree was Pastor Ron Traub at First Assembly of God. He looked at me and said "I'll say yes to that without even checking with the board or staff. I'll meet with them, of course, but I know they'll recognize, as I do, that God is at work and this is the right thing to do. I believe God will bless us for being involved."

When he said those words I felt a swell of emotion inside as this wise man with a true calling and big heart echoed what I was hoping I had communicated clearly. It seemed I was getting a glimpse into the heart of a pastor. I walked out of his office with excitement and confidence.

Next came Abiding Savior Free Lutheran, then Good News

Reformed, then other various denominations and non-denominational churches joined our cause.

It felt like God was moving, and I was just experiencing Him at work.

These churches agreed without knowing who would lead the sermon, the order of the service, the music, or the specific message. They heard my honest testimony and trusted that God would be leading their congregants to the clear Gospel message.

I remember visiting with one pastor who looked sadly at me and said, "Well, our denomination won't allow us to partner in such functions. It's against our doctrine and procedures." I understood his stance, and expected the words to come to be something along the lines of "No, I'm sorry."

But he paused and then said, "You know, I made a mistake a few years back by not getting involved in the Promise Keepers movement; I won't make that mistake again. I'm in and we'll be there."

Trust—it can be a difficult thing to give somebody. But as the recipient of these pastors' trust, I felt empowered, humbled, and more committed to God's promise of LifeLight as a binding force of His will than ever before.

Over the years, many thousands of people have surrendered their lives to Christ at the annual LifeLight community worship service. But that first year at the fairgrounds was as special and impactful as any other because it took form from a nebulous idea built around the simple concept of bringing Christians together outside the walls of church.

At the heart of most pastors is the desire to make known the Gospel of Jesus Christ.

Over 4,500 people gathered on a partly cloudy Sunday morning for that first community worship at the "Front Porch" side stage at the fairgrounds. Participating church pastors were passing out song sheets and greeting people. A local group of musicians led the songs, and KP Westmoreland, a young evangelical speaker from Oklahoma, gave the message.

I stood in the background for most of the service except for an occasional greeting with pastors and people who attended. As the small team of people who had poured their hearts into the event gathered at the back of the crowd, we all knew this was a defining moment for the festival and that there was more in store.

I believe people are hungry to experience Church.

As many left the worship time and headed for the parking lot, we could sense their enthusiasm and affirmation, but we wondered why they were leaving. We were just getting started. A little known rock band called Switchfoot would be performing at the big stage in the grandstand. These people could hear good, live music for free, and they were leaving. We realized that just as many people came only for the worship service as others were coming in after church for the rock concert. Well, we couldn't expect people to change all at once.

And I didn't expect the pastors of the various churches to give me their approval as the production crew and our committee scrambled to get ready for the bands to begin.

But they did.

To this day, the annual community worship service is one of my favorite parts of LifeLight. It's an event that's powered by the communal love of Christ in the gathering of His people and something that continues to amaze me as we witness the transformation of people's souls.

I believe people are hungry to experience Church. But, whether it's from a past experience gone bad or feeling like an outsider in a corporate worship experience, so many people hesitate to join the chorus. That's why the LifeLight community worship is so important to us; it's an opportunity for people to take part without feeling like an intruder in a closed community. It's a chance to commune with God without worrying about trying to fit into a specific group that's quite content inside its home. It's a different experience with the Lord. He really is at work, and we feel His presence when we, His people, come together.

Recently a young man and his family came up to me at a church service and shared how he surrendered to Christ at the festival church service. He has since become an ordained a pastor.

These are the stories that humble me, the ones that remind us that God is at work through LifeLight and beyond.

■ ■ ■

That first community worship service was a success, and it served as a sign of things to come as the day progressed in our new festival home.

In many ways that first year at the fairgrounds felt like our very first LifeLight festival as it resembled those other festivals we'd celebrated years earlier—like Sonshine or other national events that were cultivated on grassy hills or in concert structures. And, since it was being hosted on a truly neutral site, the crowd was more diverse than it had been on the church lawn. It also didn't hurt that we had a killer lineup featuring rising Christian bands like Salvador, LaRue, Vienna, Switchfoot, and, of course, our annual favorite, Go Fish.

I remember a family coming up to us and saying they had pitched their tent and camped at LifeLight the previous night. "We have to be the first campers for this annual festival!" Indeed they were because it was only a one-day event, and we hadn't even offered camping that year.

There was an excitement in the air and it felt good.

It also exceeded expectations as more than 10,000 people showed up for that festival.

A new day was dawning for the festival and the ministry.

■ ■ ■

A new festival location wasn't the only change God had in mind for me during 2001.

You'll hear people in the Christian faith try to tell you that you should be in a state of peace, not trying to rush through life. The more I read scripture, particularly sections about the life of the Apostle Paul and the way he was always driven to do more, I tend to doubt that more and more. We will always have peace as a follower of Jesus, that supernatural peace that comes from knowing God. But I find it's rarely a peace-from-staying-put; it's a peace born of motion. Peace as a verb.

Through all the preparations for the festival, through all the meetings with pastors to try to convince them to join our community worship, I was spending less time working at the cleaning service business that was paying my family's bills and increasingly more time doing the work of the Lord.

It became very clear to me that God wanted me to sell my business and go full time into ministry.

Even though I had heard His voice direct me toward life-changing experiences in the past and had seen how His will orchestrated LifeLight to grow into a festival that brought people toward the message of salvation, it was terrifying to think of giving up that stable income. I had a family to support, and as a businessman, there was no way I could see how to do that without a job providing some money for our livelihood.

Bowing to apprehension, I made the decision to try toughing it out by growing my business while also trying to cultivate the ministry. I even went to a Small Business Administration consultation agency for help on how to expand my business and increase cash flow so I could support my family while doing the ministry.

The consultant looked over my business and through my financial records. He asked several questions about what I did, and I did not miss the opportunity to tell him about the LifeLight festival and the mission trips we took. I'm sure I could not hide my passion, but I redirected the conversation back to the business.

He looked across the table at me and said, "I've never done this with anyone before, but I don't think you are supposed to be in business any longer. I've sat and listened to you talk about this festival and the mission trips you take, and I think you are supposed to be in full time ministry."

I'm not even sure if this man was a Christian or if he knew what he was saying, but it felt like God spoke through him that day.

Even with this apparent message from above, I still had anxiety and fear about stepping out in faith to full time ministry. Besides, how would I sell my business? Many service businesses just go away, forgotten amid the competition's availability. Why would someone buy my company when they could just start their own? I was torn; yet, I knew what was right. I just could not see it from where I was.

It became very clear to me that God wanted me to sell my business and go full time into ministry.

When I got home from that meeting, Vicki asked what had happened. She wasn't surprised at the response. She had been praying and waiting for me to come to this conclusion on my own, even though she'd probably known the answer for some time. It reminds me of Proverbs 3:5-6, "Trust in the Lord with all your heart, and lean not on your own understanding; in all your ways acknowledge Him, and He shall direct your paths."

We moved ahead with a peace that if the business sold, great. If it didn't, I would buck up and work the festival and the business. It felt like I was in two worlds, like sitting on a picket fence with one leg dangling in each property. A few months later, I was pushed off that fence into the soft grass of LifeLight. The business had sold, and we celebrated with some time off and a family trip in a newly-purchased motor home that carried us to California for a missions conference.

> Though it would seem I had learned to listen to God while shelving pride and fear, I still had to be reminded that God's plan, not mine, was the path I should be following and trusting.

Vicki and I spent days at a beautiful campus for various conference sessions with our daughters joining in a few of them. The conference teaching was challenging as well as encouraging. Each night there was praise and worship. It was just what we needed.

From California we decided to drive south and check out Mexico. We didn't know anyone there, we couldn't speak Spanish, and we didn't know where we'd stay, but I wanted to take my family on an adventure, so away we went. We happened to meet someone at a church who told us of a few places to see. What was most memorable about that trip was what Vicki called "divine appointments." Like when we ran into a few young men and one of them invited our entire family to stay at his house for a few days. We felt humbled and thankful. These men took us to visit some ministries that were making an impact in the community and also to some beautiful beaches for leisure.

It was a wonderful bonding experience for our family, just going day to day without a plan.

It was also a lesson. Though it would seem I had learned to listen to God while shelving pride and fear, I still had to be reminded that God's plan, not mine, was the path I should be following and trusting.

And during 2002's LifeLight festival that lesson came back to me.

Prior to the festival, which returned to the fairgrounds and expanded to two days, we had printed very nice souvenir programs. We planned to sell a lot of them, assuming that since everyone got to experience two days of free music, they would be able to buy a program to help cover our expenses. Over 30,000 people showed up for that weekend, but hardly anyone bought a program. The donations didn't seem to be coming in either. We were frantic, wondering what good LifeLight could be if it was so far in debt that we couldn't afford to produce a festival the next year.

I remember that sinking feeling before the Sunday morning community worship service, realizing how far we were in the financial hole. Vicki felt it too.

She had driven home that morning to pick something up, and she felt the Lord had spoken to her on the way back to the festival grounds—"Just trust Me. Why are you striving?" When she got back, she got on the pocket radios and told all of our team members to report to the main stage area immediately, regardless of what they were doing. We had to pray. She even called the people trying to sell the programs at the entrance, "Stop trying to sell them. Just give them away." She felt God had spoken to her and was wise enough to trust Him, to stop trying to "make things happen."

Gathered together on the main stage, holding hands with hearts in unison, we prayed for God to supply our needs. Here's the thing: when God guides, God provides.

Later that morning, we experienced what we consider a miracle. Over $35,000 came in during the offering at the Sunday service. The amount was more than we needed to cover our expenses. Each of us could sense God's presence as a sense of peace came over all of us and was felt about the grounds. We weren't just growing in numbers; God was changing lives.

A burden had been lifted. I wish I could say our personal finances were as smooth, but God wasn't done teaching me to trust Him.

Remember that motor home we had purchased the year before? Well, without my job and with most of my attention focused on LifeLight, I knew we would have to sell it to cover life expenses. I prayed about selling it, and God planted this thought in me, "You never asked me about buying it in the first place."

Ouch.

Isn't that how we live most of our lives? Spending time to please ourselves then pleading with God when we get into trouble? He is always a gracious and loving Father, yet; rescuing us from our life choices is in His timing and in His way.

On a Sunday almost six weeks after the festival, on October 13 to be exact, I was looking at the status of our bank accounts and wondering how we could pay our taxes, which were due in two days. A man had just looked at our motor home and said he was interested in buying it, but also said he'd have to check with a bank on financing. It didn't feel promising. And I was getting nervous. We'd written checks for our extended IRS tax date from the sale of our business, but we didn't have the money to cover them. We weren't yet paid a living wage from the ministry, but God sent me signs that gave me peace. One such sign happened when I pulled into a church parking lot to meet with a pastor while doing LifeLight work and heard the song "Where There is Faith" by 4Him. The lyrics carried peace from the speakers:

Where there is faith
There is a voice calling, keep walking
You're not alone in this world
Where there is faith
There is a peace like a child sleeping
Hope everlasting in He who is able to
Bear every Burden, to heal every hurt in my heart
It is a wonderful, powerful place
Where there is faith.

I knew God was there; He had heard my prayer. I just needed to trust Him. The next day, that guy returned with a cashier's check to buy the motor home. God is so good to us, even when our planning proves less than foolproof.

8

Keep Moving by Faith

Missions took on a new form for us in 2003 as our mentors at International Family Missions encouraged us to start taking teams down to Juarez, Mexico, on our own.

Joe Hart, IFM's late founder, seemed to see that we had our own ministry and visions and began pushing us toward independence especially during the previous year's trip when he would step back and tell us to lead various portions of the mission. At times it was intimidating, we felt unqualified—challenged. However, we felt empowered, and we trusted him. He was an incredible Godly man—Jesus worked through him and he had a soft-spoken and kind, yet strong, way about him. He absolutely loved the Mexican people and their culture and had a heart for sharing the Gospel. We tried to model our mission's ministry after his and Kathy's organization. Even though the prospect of branching out on our own was at times intimidating, we tried to model our motif after the IFM model. We loved the sincerity and respect they showed for the Mexican people and how the missionaries honored their cultural ways.

So we gathered our team, comprised of several who had joined us on prior trips along with several from our current church home, for training meetings on how to do everything from respecting the culture to sharing the Gospel. We put together crafts for women and children and hygiene packets with things like soap, toothpaste, toothbrushes, shampoo, and a Gospel tract. We learned Spanish songs and skits, and we raised money to purchase Bibles and beans and rice for food distribution.

But while we were preparing our people to succeed in a foreign land that could easily overwhelm us with the need for aid and prayer, we still had one problem to figure out: how we were going to transport this group of 40 people some 1,100 miles south?

We didn't have a bus. We didn't have a convoy of vans. And, we didn't have the money to rent something that would carry us into Juarez.

Would we dare organize a car pool and trail each other across the southwestern U.S. similar to how the wagon trains rolled across the unsettled American West?

Plus, even if we figured out how to get to Juarez, we weren't sure where we'd stay once we arrived. Previously we had crossed over the border each day and stayed at the IFM base on the U.S. side. Of course, that wasn't an option this time. As we realized the lack of a plan to get us there, I probably should have been wondering if this was meant to be. But, one of the things I've learned through my journey with Jesus is that we shouldn't waste time wondering how to do the right thing, just do it in obedience, and God will work things out for the best.

As we examined our past experiences with IFM, one of the crystalizing experiences happened while riding on that bus into Mexico. Sitting there a few feet or sometimes inches, from people we didn't know two days prior forced us to bond in a way you don't experience by traveling separately and meeting together at the destination. We laughed, cried and sweat together as the bus cruised toward the final goal. It's especially helpful for a group of Christians who often come from different denominations. The ride in close quarters allows us to get past our dogmatic differences to focus on the similarities that we share while trying to live a life for God.

By the time the bus reached Juarez, the effects of that bonding experience could be seen in how we worked together without concern or ego toward our central aim of ministering both aid and the Gospel to the people of Juarez. And once we were there, that bus served as a mobile base and a place for the team to gather or rest as we did our outreach.

So, yeah, we needed a bus.

As we finished one of our training meetings prior to the trip, I informed everyone that we knew of a church that had a coach bus for sale for $10,000. It was a substantial discount from the listed value, but that was much more money than the ministry had at the time. Even after that church agreed to lower the cost to $8,000, the price was too high for LifeLight.

Still, I didn't want to give up on the mission or the people in Juarez. While thinking about ways to get the money, I finally decided that if I could sell my family's Suburban for $5,000, we would attempt to buy the bus. We still had no idea who would drive it, but we prayed about the situation and left it in God's hands.

The next day, after a Sunday church service, we were asked to lunch by one of the families scheduled to be part of our mission trip. During the meal, they handed us a check for $8,000, the exact amount we needed to buy the bus. We were totally shocked as a range of emotions from graciousness to humility flowed through us. As if that wasn't spectacular enough, we returned home to find a message on our answering machine from another family who wanted to buy our Suburban specifically because they knew it would help fund the bus purchase.

That message was followed by a call from a man who had been on a mission trip with us in the past and just happened to be a well-qualified bus driver. He could get the time off to be our primary driver on our next trip and wanted to guide us into Mexico.

We even had someone give us a gift to cover the insurance for the bus for an entire year—everything was being covered, even the things we hadn't considered.

It was a streak of blessings that was almost overwhelming. Though as they say on those late night infomercials while hocking products no one ever needs, "but wait…there's more!"

That evening the phone rang again. It was Vicki's parents asking us to come over to meet with Vicki's aunt, who was in town. She wanted to talk to us.

> It was a streak of blessings that was almost overwhelming.

When we met, she informed us she didn't know anything about commercial buses, but she wanted to give us her car so we would have something to drive in the event that we sold our Suburban to help fund our adventure south. And with that she handed us the keys to her 1989 Oldsmobile. That car was one of the most reliable vehicles we have ever owned, and we were even able to extend its blessing by giving it to a family when we didn't need it any more.

What a crazy, wonderful, day. In just 24 hours we had gone

from wondering if this mission trip was going to be financially feasible to having enough money to cover the purchase of the bus, the first year's insurance, and to get all the urgent repair issues handled. We even had enough to have the bus re-lettered with the LifeLight logo.

It reminded me, and all of us, what God is capable of if you put trust into His plan. It wasn't the last time we had to rely on His plan on this mission.

■ ■ ■

Two weeks out from the trip, the director of an orphanage in Juarez we had arranged for the team to stay at called with a prayer request.

He told us that hundreds of people who had been living on vacant land in pallet and cardboard homes had been driven off the property. The local police, under the direction of a Mexican factory, had raided the spot in the middle of the night, kicking people off the land and setting fire to the modest, makeshift homes. Some of those dwellings had propane tanks and when met with the fire, they exploded to cause even more damage to the property and the people. Some of those people, including children, died and many more were injured. The majority of these squatters lost everything in the flames.

I don't pretend to know the politics of the situation but our hearts went out to these families who, like tens of thousands of people in Juarez, lived in those shanty towns that were so easily destroyed.

The orphanage director didn't know where these displaced people had gone. Juarez didn't have the local government or charitable aid organizations swooping in to save the day with temporary lodging, food, and relief funds. The people were on their own. The orphanage director said they needed our help, even if we didn't quite know how to help them.

We all prayed about how we might facilitate a happy ending to a tragic story.

This development underscored why we were making this journey to Juarez. But it also reaffirmed something I felt was necessary after we decided to begin our mission trips—to ensure the safety and well-being of the people we were charged to lead. As a result, we devised three non-negotiable rules that we had to follow once we crossed the border into Mexico.

The first, we would always arrive in Mexico before dark. This rule applied to the bus or a car. With a 2-hour drive to the orphanage from the border crossing it was in our best interest to do this, as it is not always safe to drive after sunset in many third world countries. Though, to be fair, it's not safe to drive in many part of the United States after dark.

The second rule, if anyone in our group became sick, we would bypass the Mexican medical facilities in favor of taking the injured party back to U.S. for treatment. This was for liability issues and insurance, but mostly a decision based on the quality of care.

We devised three non-negotiable rules that we had to follow once we crossed the border into Mexico.

The third rule, team members would never split up while in Mexico. It's just not a good idea in a part of a country ruled by drug cartels with a reputation for kidnapping tourists.

We felt confident that if we held true to each of these three rules our chances for safety and fulfillment of the mission would increase exponentially.

And yet, all three of these basic safety principles were

violated the first night of our first LifeLight-organized mission trip. And broken by us, the leaders, no less!

It started with breaking the first rule after we fell behind schedule during our 26-hour ride from Sioux Falls. As a result, it was dark when we rolled the LifeLight bus into Mexico with a two-hour drive ahead of us to reach the orphanage. We had considered staying in Fabens or El Paso, Texas, until the next morning. But the drive had been long, and our people were exhausted. We thought it would be better for them if we pushed forward toward the orphanage. The decision was rationalized with the fact that a friend who lived in El Paso would be escorting us as we followed his car through the Mexican part of the journey. Of course, this meant we had to try to keep up with him as he wove through traffic like a car running from police in one of those cheesy '80's cop shows.

The traffic was just one of many things our missionaries had to adjust to in this new country. Among the differences was the stark confrontation with our own mortality. I'll never forget the fear in our team, many of whom had never been on a mission trip prior to this, as the bus navigated a U-turn to get back on the right path. The maneuver gave us a clear view of a dead body lying on the side of the road. I don't know how the person died, but the corpse was a jarring reminder that this place was far from home. And that I had already broken the first rule in our marching orders to safety. (Don't drive after dark in Mexico).

It was midnight when we arrived at the orphanage and were greeted with a great sense of relief. We had been on that bus for more than two days, and it felt good to be off of it, setting up temporary lodging in something that didn't have wheels and the constant motion of traveling.

The respite didn't last long.

About an hour later, the one-and-a-half-year-old daughter

of one of our missionary team members began having trouble breathing. Vicki was concerned so we spoke with the girl's family and made the decision that she had to see a doctor. Her name was Hannah and her lungs sounded so congested that we weren't sure there was time to drive her two hours or more to the perceived safety of a hospital in America. We decided to break rule number two, and let a man named Paco drive us to a Mexican doctor.

At this point, we didn't feel like very qualified leaders as we helplessly rode in a beat-up Dodge Caravan accompanying Hannah, her parents, and another team member who was a nurse, en route to medical aid.

Paco, who was a man of faith, navigated us to the clinic where they had to call the doctor in from his home. Once he arrived, the doctor took one look at Hannah and told us to get her over the border to an American hospital as soon as possible.

Good advice. The only problem was the nearest border crossing was closed, which meant we would have to drive the rural highway back to the Juarez/El Paso crossing. That could take an extra hour or more. We didn't really have a choice; Hannah needed medical attention, and the only one who was qualified to do anything in this Mexican city just told us to get into America. We rushed off toward the U.S. praying for angels of safety and healing. They certainly were looking after us as we made it across the border without incident or proper documentation.

Hannah needed some time in the hospital, but we were told the next day she would be okay. Her father, Bret, my friend and fellow evangelist, came back into Mexico the next day so he could talk with the orphaned Mexican kids while his daughter lay in a hospital bed. I was overwhelmed with awe and admiration that Bret came back to share the story of Hannah's struggle the night before.

From there, thank God, our mission trip progressed as planned; we played with the children in the orphanage and continued house visitations and Bible club outreaches. Part of that plan was keeping Thursday open as a flex day, of sorts, where the only scheduled guidance was "no plan." It was difficult for me and the other team members as we wanted to fill every minute and every second of our time there trying to extend some aid, hope, or God's message to the people of Mexico. But, both Vicki and I believed God was telling us to leave this Thursday open. So we did. Deep down we were hoping to find the fire victims.

What happened next is something I had never seen before and have not seen since.

After loading up the bus that Thursday morning, we told the team, "Whatever God puts in our path today, that's what we are doing."

I'm sure quite a few of us expected to spend the day driving in circles around the Mexican border towns.

With our Mexican translators in tow, we drove the bus to the east side of Juarez where the horrendous fire had destroyed the pallet homes we had been praying about. The bus stopped there and we got out and walked around the charred landscape littered with remnants of what little possessions these families had—toys, mattresses and propane tanks. We prayed as we walked the open field of desert that resembled a massive war zone of abandoned debris and dashed dreams.

From there we drove up and down some dirt paths that served as default streets in this former shanty town. We had sack lunches with us that day, as well as some supplies to do our various ministries. After driving the area a bit, the bus pulled over for a lunch break. What happened next is something I had never seen before and have not seen since.

Now, you have to understand that when an American bus enters the poorer areas of Mexico, it naturally draws a crowd. But the situation in this destroyed area was much different than that.

As we began to get our lunches out to eat on the bus, a group of Mexicans, mostly families, formed a semi-circle around the bus and stood there, just waiting, as if they had known we were supposed to meet them at that very location.

I stepped off the bus with our translator and asked him to find out what was happening. When he returned to relay the information, his face was grave. "Alan, these are the people who were in the fire; they are ones who lost everything."

> Listening to the Holy Spirit and taking the church outside the walls was a much better strategy than anything we could have come up with.

Immediately, in my broken Spanish, I said, "We are from the United States of America. We prayed that we would find you, and we would like to spend time with you. We have things for the children, and our ladies would like to spend time with your ladies. We have a Bible study for the men."

At that point a young man walked out into the center of the crowd and said, "Mi nombre es Jorge," then he switched to English, and though his speech patterns were broken, his words were very clear, "Two weeks ago we lost everything in a fire, and I dropped to my knees in this very spot and said, 'God, you know our needs. Please send help!'" He paused with emotion before continuing, "And here you are, my friends. Here you are!"

Meanwhile on the bus, the team was filled with emotion. They couldn't eat their lunches and decided to give them away. They were crying and seemed paralyzed for quite a period of time before they could even get off the bus.

Jorge and his wife Luz were living in a pallet home with a blanket for a door. They invited us into their house that day. Jorge played the guitar; he was a talented musician. Luz served us delicious Mexican food. It was such a precious gesture, dipping into the little that they had to serve us, their guests. We sat speechless as we took in the state of their life and the stories they told us about their daily struggles, such as where their next meal would come from. But God provided, they assured us. I wondered what God was going to do. I should have known that He had a plan for Jorge and for us as this encounter would pave the way for many future mission trips to Mexico. Many miraculous things happened on that trip—a marriage was healed and we saw the beginning of several life long friendships with our new Hispanic friends.

Since that meeting we continued to lead trips into Mexico, and Jorge has always been there helping and serving alongside us. We sponsored him in Bible school a few years later and attended his graduation. Today, Jorge is a pastor and he lives with his family near the U.S. border. He even planted a LifeLight church in his neighborhood where he ministered to the neighboring families in Juarez as they battled through the constant danger and fear of the ongoing Mexican drug war with the cartels—a war that you should realize is fueled by the American appetite for drugs.

Jorge has many times reminded me that we serve the King of Kings, and if God wants to use him here on Earth, it's here he will stay. And if he is to die, then he will be with Jesus in Heaven. He served on the frontlines in Mexico, reaching and rescuing many with the love and grace of Jesus. I am unashamed to tell you that he is my modern day hero. I know it was not by chance that we met him all those years ago during that whimsical February day in 2003.

Leaving our new-found friends behind, we all felt somber and broken that day, feeling inadequate to the needs that were before us. It was, once again, in that moment that we realized how divine the hand of God was in our decision to have a day without a plan. Listening to the Holy Spirit and taking the church outside the walls was a much better strategy than anything we could have come up with.

9

Divine Encounters–Living Your Call

Though meeting Jorge was an encounter that deepened our faith and our commitment to helping the people of Juarez, he was just one of many people we met in 2003 who had a major impact on the development of LifeLight.

That April, shortly after that memorable Mexico trip, Vicki and I trekked to the Gospel Music Association week in Nashville. It was a chance to scout for potential bands to add to the next LifeLight festival. It was also an opportunity to meet and network with some of the best in the contemporary Christian music world.

Vicki and I always pray for divine appointments, and this day was no different as we began our day asking God for guidance as we met people, spoke with vendors, and sat through seminars and tracts for concert promoters.

One morning we attended a breakfast featuring Luis Palau,

the famed evangelist who shares Christ through crusades and festivals all over the world. Luis has a following of people with enough ardent support that they'll fill their front lawns with "Luis Palau" signs in promotion of his festivals. During his talk he had most of the audience in stiches because of his transparent sense of humor and an energy that belies his age. Luis has a passion for relevant mass evangelism that effectively reaches people with the Gospel. His hope and encouragement for those of us in the room to affect the next generation was contagious.

Afterward, Palau was swarmed with people greeting him or trying to get his attention. We waited for our own audience with him and promptly told him about our little, but growing festival in Sioux Falls. We didn't mess around and plainly asked him to speak at LifeLight. Palau looked at us with his winsome smile and told us he'd love to. We were elated. It almost seemed too easy.

Next in line was his son, Kevin, who is now a wise resource and good friend. Kevin is the more pragmatic part of the Palau clan. That morning after Luis made a commitment to us, Kevin brought us down to reality by saying he'd check his father's schedule for us because Luis didn't really keep track of it. As it turned out, he wasn't available in 2003. But that morning started a long relationship with the Luis Palau Evangelistic Association. And, he did speak at LifeLight, but not until 2005. It was worth the wait as the festival crowd responded with enthusiasm to his message. He even returned the next year in 2006.

Still charged from the positive result of the Palau meeting, we continued our day in Nashville by walking up to Jon and Sherry Rivers, who were morning show hosts for the worldwide Christian radio network K-LOVE. The station played the bands that populated our LifeLight lineups, everything from the young rock bands to the more contemporary Gospel acts. Of course, both Jon and Sherry are loved and respected by the bands and artists they have worked with through their years in radio.

Just like we did with the Palau's, we walked straight to them and shared what God was doing in South Dakota. We personally invited the Rivers to come and observe the festival firsthand, even suggested that they broadcast live from LifeLight.

Almost instantly after making the offer I started thinking, "Are we brave or tactless?" Then, I started wondering how they would react to the bold invites. I don't know what they saw in us that day. Maybe they simply heard and followed God's leading because they also said yes and came to Sioux Falls that Labor Day weekend. Through their connection to K-LOVE, they were also instrumental in K-LOVE's future partnership with LifeLight and the expansion of our national presence through their broadcasting.

Looking back on that first meeting in Nashville, it felt like we had known the Rivers forever. We instantly clicked and bonded over our devotion to Christ.

We came away from the GMA week with several wonderful lifelong friends. But we also left with some observations about the contemporary Christian music realm.

First, it was difficult not to notice the unity and respect among the musicians, regardless of genre. Rather than focus on dividing factors like genre styles, age, or fashion aesthetics, these musicians chose to bond over their similarities in living life through Jesus' lead.

The other takeaway was that we became a little uncomfortable with some people and practices in the Christian music industry. Now, I have to offer the caveat that this observation wasn't universal. Most of the people we met and have worked with have a sincere passion for God and His divine plan. But, in the midst of the business side of the Christian music industry, there was a contrast to the mission conference we had been to earlier. That mission conference was bathed in prayer, and you would always see people reading their Bibles and seeking God for the future direction of their ministries. It was something we felt was lacking at the GMA gathering.

I believe in asking for God's direction and divine guidance for many facets of life, especially with major life or ministry decisions. And, as Christians in an industry with the sole purpose of producing and booking Christian artists, I think we should stand out in contrast to any of the worldly business models.

If we even flirt with the idea of hypocrisy, our mission can be tainted by the denouncements of people who are just waiting for prominent Christians to make a misstep in their walk of faith.

One conversation that has stuck in my mind to this very day took place when Vicki and I were visiting with a leading Nashville agent who asked why we kept the LifeLight festival free of charge. He immediately quipped, "For me, it's all about ticket sales and making money."

Oh really? We felt saddened as he obviously didn't understand our calling—to share the Good News of Jesus Christ to the masses. We have no problem with ticket sales; however, the disappointment for us was that we were at a Gospel music event that, at times, was trumpeting some rather secular goals. As Christians, our aim should never be the profit, but obedience to the call of Christ.

This conversation was a reminder to me of what God had called us to do with LifeLight. The festival and the ministry has to be more than a business production that happens to have Christian music on stage. I once heard someone excuse the behavior of a Christian band's manager by saying, "That's just business, and it's just the way it is done." My internal reaction was, "No! We do ministry, not business." Our ministry should include good, moral business practices. In every transaction we must never take off our ministry hats. It's who we are as disciples of Christ, and it is who we are as we claim to be part of a Christian music ministry. It's part of the reason why the banner we place above the main stage at LifeLight each year reads, "To God be the Glory."

There was a sense of irony in feeling out-of-place because of my faith at a gathering of Christian artists, promoters, and business people. Prior to devoting my life's work to LifeLight, I had actually become comfortable in the secular business world with being vocal and open about my faith. Yet, there I was, in a Christian setting surrounded by people who supposedly shared my beliefs, feeling shamed for wanting to uphold my Christian ethics in the "business" part of our ministry.

> Our aim should never be the profit, but obedience to the call of Christ.

My desire with LifeLight has always been to remain faithful to the ministry's calling because all any of us do is God's work and that can be taken away at any time by actions that refute God's will.

Though my experiences with this form of hypocrisy were surprising, they didn't taint the amazing experiences we had meeting many truly humble, passionate believers in Christ and in meeting friends who have helped make our bond with Christ even stronger.

■ ■ ■

Sometimes you seek out divine encounters, other times they come to you. Sometimes they arrive in the form of a big, purple bus.

I was at the festival grounds working prep for the 2003 festival when a rambling, purple Bluebird bus with the words "Mother Load" painted on the front of it pulled up. Instantly, I admired its unconventional appearance.

As I walked toward the bus a nice-looking family of six casually stepped out of the bus and came toward me as if we had an appointment. The father, a guy named Tony, introduced himself with a firm handshake, a warm smile, and the simple question of "What do you have going on here?" In my mind, the better question was, "What are you doing here?" But, I've come to learn that God delivers help in many forms.

At the time, the family was a resident of the road, traveling all over the U.S. as missionaries using the bus as their mobile church. During their ventures they would help others along the path, many times staying in a city or area for as long as was needed. That mantra was why they had driven their unique bus to Sioux Falls and searched us out; they wanted to volunteer at LifeLight in any way they could.

I was blown away. We were less than eight weeks from the festival and barely treading water, so to speak, as we tried to handle the current of planning, preparing, and constructing our annual music festival.

That year was crucial for us as we had expanded the festival to three days, running Friday through Sunday of Labor Day weekend. We had expanded the festival's scope by jumping up to six stages of live music and speakers. We also took on a much larger budget, all as a circumstance of faith. The festival was about to evolve in 2003, and God was preparing us for it.

Tony's experience as a contractor coupled with his teaching and missions experiences as a pastor were God's gift to us at that time as he and his family helped take our festival to the next level by coordinating the logistical litany of fencing, construction, parking, portable toilet placement, electrical requirements, tents, tables, chairs, booth rentals and more.

■ ■ ■

The 2003 LifeLight festival was an amazing feat to watch as more than 110,000 people poured into the fairgrounds over three days. Our lineup featured bands at the top of the Christian music scene—from the rock of Newsboys, Skillet, and Audio Adrenaline to the pop sounds of Rebecca St James, Geoff Moore, and many others. We even included Gospel and coffeehouse stages, as well as the ever-popular "Souled Out" stage with its variety of hard-core, screamo bands.

Once again, the community worship service proved to be the spiritual highlight, greater than the numbers are the testimonies like this one. As thousands packed into the grandstand to hear the music and the message presented by the young evangelist Jose Zayas, there were men like Mike who gave his life to Christ that year. Mike was on a journey and God used LifeLight at the right time for him to take the next step

Mike was a man who had been contemplating suicide for months. He knew he needed to commit his life to Jesus to find peace. For weeks and weeks, he and his wife had been searching for a church to join when they decided to check out the LifeLight festival, thinking they'd hear some bands and maybe find a church that suited them.

During the first two days of the festival Mike heard calls to accept Jesus as he walked past prayer tents and stages. He said he'd think, "Now is the time," but still not act on the feeling. By Sunday morning, he was part of the thousands of people at that community worship service with Jose Zayas, finding his spirit being moved as the audience sang together—knowing they were standing together because they loved Jesus.

Mike began singing along and taking in the experience when

two people sitting on a grassy berm caught his eye. One was a casually dressed man in his 50s. Five feet from him was a teenager wearing baggy black pants and matching shirt. A chain wallet was hanging from his pockets. They looked vastly different, but as they sang the same songs together, Mike realized they were connected by the bond of loving Jesus.

After the singing was over, Zayas took over the stage. This is when Mike's memory gets a little fuzzy.

"My mind was racing. I tried to listen to Jose's message," Mike told me later. "I kept thinking of the two men below. Then I would tune into Jose again. And again, I would think of the men below. I wanted to share in what they had. Then, I got the chance… Jose asked everyone to stand and close his or her eyes. He said, 'If you are ready to accept Jesus as your Lord and Savior raise your hand.' My wife and I were holding hands at the time; I let go and raised my arm as high as I could. No matter how hard I stretched I couldn't seem to raise my hand high enough. Next, Jose told everyone to lower their hands and open their eyes. He then asked everyone who had raised their hands to make their way to the stage as soon as the next song began. Without saying a word or even looking at each other, my wife and I scooped up our belongings to begin walking toward the stage. Once the group gathered at the stage, we were directed toward the prayer tent where volunteers waited to pray with us."

Inside the tent Mike and his wife, still holding hands, dropped to their knees and prayed aloud confessing their sins, accepting Jesus as Lord and Savior, asking the Holy Spirit to enter their lives and be their guide.

Mike was told by a prayer leader to say what was in his heart.

He thanked God for saving him, for seeking him when he would not seek Jesus. For finding him after he, time and time again, wandered away. For pulling him out of the darkness when he could not find his own way. He thanked God for giving him a great family, friends, and a wonderful wife who always supported him.

With tears in his eyes, Mike's doubt was gone, and by God's grace he had been saved.

At the closing concert that Sunday night the grandstand area was packed with hardly any room to stand as the Newsboys ran through a set of their dynamic rock tunes. It was amazing to watch as this mass of people moved, swayed, and jumped almost as one under the direction of this band they were so excited to see. As far as numbers go, this wasn't too unusual for the fairgrounds as the grandstand had hosted the likes of Christina Aguilera and 'N Sync with all their screaming fans during the late '90s heyday of teen pop. But as the 2003 LifeLight festival unfolded, the fair and county officials were scratching their heads in wonderment at how this concert was so different than the usual fairgrounds affair accompanied by impolite behavior, injuries and sometimes arrests.

One of the fair's operations guys came up to me the night of the Newsboys performance. He was a very straight-forward fellow who often said what he thought, sometimes in a way that you may not like. He looked at me with emotion in his eyes that night and told me, "In all my years of running fairs and watching people, I have never seen anything like this. All these people having fun and with no arrests or obnoxious behavior." He said he would not have believed you could get this many people on the grounds for a rock concert without seeing the effects of underage drinking or fighting. "You name it, I've seen it all," he said. "This is a very good event you have going, and I can say from experience that there are over 30,000 people in the grandstand for this show alone."

It was music to my ears. A tune that built joy in my heart, not just from the affirmation that we were producing a safe event that could inspire people toward salvation, but also that LifeLight was attracting the kind of numbers that could put it on the national map of Christian events. Drawing more than 110,000 over the course of the 2003 festival made us one of the largest Christian festivals in America. It brought us a type of awareness that could draw attention from various national musicians, promoters, speakers, and churches. It was also confirmation that we were making a difference, the way God had intended. Though, tripling in size from the 32,000 attendees we had the year before did present its own problems going into 2004.

While preparing for that 2004 festival we received a call from a city official telling us that we had too many people for the grandstand area to house the main stage. He said that large of a crowd compromised the safety of everyone involved. This wouldn't normally be a big problem as we could just plan to position a stage in a more open part of the fairgrounds. But, the fair had since changed management, which meant we had to establish a new level of trust with these people, many of whom had never been to a LifeLight festival.

We looked at the grounds and suggested using a nearby field for the location of the main stage and using the grandstand area as a complementary stage. We were certain the festival was going to get bigger as we decided to make it a four day event in 2004, so we proposed bringing in dirt and planting grass in that open field to make the environment more comfortable for the audience. The new fair leadership might have found it odd that we, facility renters, were leading the charge on improving their property. Typically, it takes a committee or two to get these things done in the world of bureaucracy. But, we just charged right in with blue-prints and a vision. After the meeting they agreed to our plans, and we were off and running, again.

The plan was on course, but even as visionaries, we could not have predicted what happened next.

We pulled out all the stops for that 2004 festival; our big dreams were finally becoming realized as we began loading up those six stages with first class acts. There was a country Gospel stage featuring Larry Gatlin. The young Chris Tomlin was leading our Coffeehouse stage. The Souled Out stage was moved to the grandstand, which became a festival of its own when acts like the crossover rock band Blindside played. We paired that stage with an area for BMX trick riders and skateboarders. We even had a motocross demo team literally jumping across part of the Souled Out stage as bands performed. And on our main stage, the one that was becoming so favored that it outgrew the fairgrounds' grandstand, we welcomed headliners Steven Curtis Chapman and the rising rock band Casting Crowns, both attracting a mass of fans. We also welcomed Christian speakers like Dr. James Dobson of Focus on the Family and K.P. Yohannan of Gospel for Asia.

My daughters were now in high school, and the oldest had graduated. It seemed like time had flown by. They were busy like everyone with assigned duties at the festival, but this year I had dropped way back on asking much from them. After all, we finally had some paid staff and a very capable volunteer team. I did have one memorable moment as our youngest daughter, the redhead, ran from Souled Out stage to the backstage area of main stage where the temporary campers were placed for us to sleep in, for dressing rooms, and for our guests to hang out in. We had assigned the same camper we were using at night to Dr. Dobson to use during the day. As she barreled past me and headed for the door of a camper a strong gentleman, who happened to be Dr. Dobson's security, was standing by the camper door and stopped her, saying, 'Young lady…you can't go in there. This is

Dr. Dobson's camper.' She looked at him and said, "Who is he?!... This is my camper, and I need my sneakers now. Blindside goes on stage any minute! I have to have them." She proceeded in and left with her sneakers, heading to the mosh pit. We got a laugh out of it and were a bit embarrassed as we had raised our daughters while listening to Focus on the Family and reading several parenting books by Dr. Dobson. This would end up being a bit of humor needed in what was to come.

The drama had begun, and we were not prepared for the increased complications that came from expanding this festival. Though, not all of them were our fault.

We had presented plans and designs for a beautiful grass field to the fairgrounds' board and negotiated a partnership with the county and the city to accomplish this vision before the 2004 festival. By mid-summer no dirt had been moved or grass seeded. In fact, we had to plead to get the fair's help and approval for everything from mosquito spraying to Department of Transportation signage, and it seemed like we were making little progress. As I look back on this now, I realize we had not taken the appropriate steps to build relationships with the city and the county, and as a result, they had no clear understanding of how large LifeLight was to become. The city hosted a free jazz and blues festival every summer, but that was a different animal, so to speak. LifeLight was evolving into something Sioux Falls had never seen before—in terms of size and scope. The city, the county, and those of us in LifeLight weren't as prepared for it as we should have been. Still, the support the city would normally give an event like this wasn't coming, and we were caught in what seemed to be a turf war between the city and the county because of the fairgrounds' zoning issues.

To make the preparation worse, we had a lot of pre-fest rain, which made all landscaping and set-up even more challenging in fields that were now closer to sprawling pads of mud than acres of rain-soaked lawns. The idea of people standing, dancing, and walking back and forth in these fields wasn't just messy; it was becoming a liability. So with only a few days to go before the festival started, we made the decision to put the stage on the fairgrounds' asphalt parking lot and use those fields for parking.

We called on a faithful friend of ours who had a sod lawn business and asked him to start laying squares of that lush, vibrant green grass on the dark, hard asphalt of the lot. It looked so bizarre, as if they were trying to hide the crust of urban sprawl under nature, but it worked. Even though it was taking place on a lake of asphalt, we had a nice field of grass in front of the main stage.

People were intrigued and amazed when they arrived and saw all the lush grass on the blacktop parking lot, and at the same time, some of those people might have wondered if I was crazy. In retrospect, part of my pride had gotten in the way over the sod issue. I knew the grass would be no good after the festival was completed, but I made it clear to people that we had envisioned and promised a field of grass. And, by golly, we got it! Plus, it was difficult to imagine thousands of people standing on smelting hot asphalt while worshipping God.

That first day of the 2004 festival, the crowd numbers were swelling; more people came in than even we had expected. As the people streamed into the fairgrounds, we had to make adjustments on the fly. Our campgrounds quickly became full, so we had to find additional areas for people to set up camp. Parking was already strained due to the decision to take up part of the lot for the main stage area, so traffic backed up and overflowed into nearby residential areas. By late Saturday night, the local media was announcing on TV that the fairgrounds were too crowded to accommodate any more traffic. I think this only helped us attract more people as normal curiosity compelled people to check out the scene.

When it was over, the fair officials counted 240,000 people over the four days. It was more than double the previous year's attendance.

The increased crowds and associated problems caused stress on all of us, particularly our unpaid volunteer staff. You could see it on their faces, as they were no longer having fun, but were frantically working to handle the large crowd. I realized the responsibilities we had put on them were too great; we overwhelmed the facilities, and there was no real way to control everything with our limited group of helpers.

As the festival progressed through the years, we needed the Sunday morning church service offering to help fund our free festival. In spite of how tired our staff was, we were all looking for that Sunday morning service to enrich us, and help pay for this festival which had budgeted for over $500,000. Then, in the middle of our outdoor church service, it started raining. Not just a gentle rain to cool us all off, but a massive downpour from one of those classic Great Plains thunderstorms that turn the entire horizon into an ominous blue-gray mass crackling with electricity and grunting thunder. I watched as the clouds continued to roll our way, hitting us with a monsoon of moisture as people started running to their cars to seek shelter. We hadn't even had time to take the morning offering before we all got soaked.

However, not everyone had run to their cars; Jose Zayas was still on stage preaching as the rain poured. And people were standing there listening to his message.

As the rain subsided, we surveyed the situation. There was water everywhere, and the power cables running to the main stage were literally under water. A stagehand walked the roof of the stage to push water off with large squeegees. On the ground, people were still huddled under tarps, rain gear, and umbrellas in the muddy sod—or what was left of it. It was a wet mess.

We discussed the merits of resuming the service versus ending it and moving on toward the rest of the day. Ultimately, we decided to restart the worship service and see how many people would return.

From the main stage I looked out at the crowd to see many huddled on the soggy sod that had now meshed into the asphalt parking lot pavement. Thousands of others still stood underneath tarps and blankets. With their focus on me, I began to chant, "God is good!" And the audience responded, "All the time!"

"All the time," I yelled. They responded, "God is good!"

The bantering volleyed back and forth between the crowd and I when a beautiful rainbow streaked against the background. The sight caused the crowd to erupt with screams of delight. It was an emotional high I will never forget, one that also gave our team of volunteers the confidence to keep going, albeit without the boost of the Sunday morning offering we were accustomed to. With all the chaos and scrambling to make sure the festival would go on, it just did not seem like a good time to start passing buckets around and ask for money. God knew our needs, and He was in control.

With all the chaos and scrambling to make sure the festival would go on, it just did not seem like a good time to start passing buckets around and ask for money.

After some fast track rearranging of the bands by reassigning stages to make up for the weather delay, we pressed on through the festival's final day. That night I watched as Mark Hall of Casting Crowns shared the Gospel story with an audience of about 70,000 people and related it to his own life. Jorge, our missionary friend from Mexico, was there with tears streaming down his face as we watched people surrender everything to Christ. The chains of abuse, bad marriages, depression, drugs, alcohol, and suicidal thoughts were all given up in a large parking lot so full of people there was only room to stand. Many prayed in the crowd with our prayer partners, many entered the prayer tent in the distance, and many stood in the crowd with their hands raised as Mark Hall asked if they wanted to give up everything and commit their lives to Jesus. All was quiet as you could feel God's presence moving into peoples' lives.

10

We're Moving to a Water park?

Our 2004 festival had lifted us to a new stratosphere of success as the 240,000 people we drew made LifeLight the largest Christian music festival in America, bigger than many stable festivals which had been around since the early '80s.

We believed the combination of excellent musical acts, honest testimonials, and the simple fact that we didn't charge for the event combined to make it a truly special gathering. People traveled through several states to be part of this event that was barely on the national media radar.

In many ways, it had become everything we envisioned. And yet, the success of LifeLight's evolution was also the biggest detriment to its future stability.

Despite attracting the second largest single event audience in the state of South Dakota after the annual Sturgis Motorcycle

Rally, LifeLight couldn't turn a profit.

After the paying the expenses of our staff and the various festival expenditures, LifeLight was $100,000 in debt. The larger the festival grew, the more it cost; and freewill offerings were not keeping up with the costs. Part of what got us into financial trouble from the 2004 festival was my desire to, perhaps, do too much in one year. We went to a four-day festival and added top caliber bands in every genre. My vision and desire for that year's festival was so big that it included the production of a reality video dubbed "The Making of a Free Festival." It was probably a few years ahead of its time.

All of this coupled with the loss of the Sunday worship service offerings and weather-related issues caused a financial shortfall that revealed our infrastructure shortcomings.

We needed more sponsors. But, attracting them was difficult because there was still some confusion as to what LifeLight was and where it came from. After the festival ended I actually heard some people say, "I hope LifeLight comes back to Sioux Falls next year." They truly thought we were a traveling festival that migrated from town to town spreading the message of God. I don't know if they didn't read the literature around the festival or didn't pay attention to what we said from the stage, but somehow the simplest parts of our information weren't registering with the very people we were ministering to.

It was frustrating. And if the people who attended the festival didn't know about its local ties it was easy to assume the folks in the local business world, who were our potential sponsors, were also in the dark about our base of operations and our overall mission.

Obviously, we needed to commit to a more focused effort to effectively communicate who we were and what we did.

With an operating budget in the red, that wasn't going to be an easy task to accomplish. Marketing costs money. And the media, while they were supportive in covering LifeLight, was more interested in asking about our financial state than publishing reports that would help ease the confusion of what we were.

One solution suggested we put the festival on hold for a year until we became more financially stable. We never entertained the idea. Our journey had shown us, over and over again, that walking in faith would supply the means to continue the trek. We were confident the money would come one way or another. So Vicki and I, along with a few loyal team members, began plotting the next year's festival—even though we were still trying to pay for the past one.

We started early meetings with the fairgrounds' staff, but as we discussed returning to the location that was built more for 4-H shows than a sprawling music festival, it became abundantly clear that we had outgrown the setting. Vicki and I kept thinking, "This was not the original dream and vision."

When we plotted the blueprints of this festival, we saw fields of grass, not outdated fairgrounds with an infrastructure set up for livestock and carnival equipment. We prayed on the situation and soon knew we had to find a new home for LifeLight, and it had to be for the next festival. But this wasn't quite the time to spring that development. First, we needed to formulate a plan to pay our bills because the financial uncertainty was causing stress in the LifeLight ranks.

Our journey had shown us, over and over again, that walking in faith would supply the means to continue the trek.

Through board meetings and sessions designed to brainstorm any ways to remedy our debts we heard the familiar call to charge an entry fee to the LifeLight festival.

"Why should it be free?" asked some people within the church. "Just charge a ticket price, even a few dollars per person. $80 or $80 would still be cheaper than any other event like this and will help immensely."

The arguments seemed logical as a means to an end of these problems. But we knew adding an entry fee would dishonor our calling. We had to obey God's direction to take the church outside the walls, and a fundamental aspect of church is that people don't have to buy tickets to walk into a service. We had to keep the LifeLight festival as open and welcoming as church. Our desire was that the Christians would fund the event so that all could come and experience it, especially those outside the Christian faith who would never walk through the doors of a church, but would certainly frequent concerts.

We just had to keep focused on the road ahead and beware of the real enemy.

Despite my convictions, I felt responsible for the shortfalls.

On top of my doubts, there was dissention in our group that I couldn't recognize. A faithful friend had to pull me aside and open my eyes to the problem: some members of our team believed they could take over and run the operation better.

The friend who alerted me of the internal schism told me, "You need to make decisions on things sooner rather than later about who is on this team." Those words were hard for me to digest, so difficult in fact that I began to question my ability as a leader or a coach. Part of my pain came from understanding that our core team that had worked so hard to make LifeLight an unexpected success was splintering apart. But it made me seriously consider if I was the problem. At times my self-doubt and despair coaxed me into thinking I would have been better off going back into a "normal" job and letting someone else make the tough decisions. Through it all, Vicki was heartbroken.

Fortunately, and in spite of my doubts, this was God's event and He is always faithful.

We had a very wise board and pastoral counsel that enabled us to weather the storm; during this difficult season they continued to encourage, challenge, and support us. We love all those who may differ with our philosophy in ministry and believe the body of Christ is diverse. In fact, that diversity is one of the Church's strengths. But not all people are yoked to travel together. I finally understood that concept when I recalled a prophecy that was given to us in the early years of LifeLight.

Friends who had traveled with us on our first mission trip had come to us to share what they believed God had spoken to them about LifeLight. They said our ministry would be like that of a stagecoach with Vicki and I as the drivers. There would be a great team that would go to many great places with us. Some would need to be retired along the way and more would join on. Some would be with us for a short duration, some the long haul. The coach would also be full of people. We couldn't be discouraged about changing "horses" or, at times, the route. We just had to keep focused on the road ahead and beware of the real enemy who would like to stop the stagecoach entirely.

After the internal struggles came to pass, about 15 people had left the team.

That prophecy about the stagecoach has been an encouragement over the years because sometimes the hardest thing to do is "change horses." Many get weary along the way and many are only here for a season; some will be along for the entire ride. Meanwhile, we're so thankful for all of those who got us where we are today. It's worth remembering that last thought, especially in times of turmoil.

In January of 2005, while Vicki and I were sitting in a board meeting about the ministry's debts, our good friend, Lynn, was in the hospital fighting cancer. Lynn and her husband were dear friends with whom we cherished many memories. In her last days they had spent countless hours in the hospital ministering to others during their own times of trial and pain.

During our meeting we received the phone call that the cancer had taken its toll; she was on her deathbed. We replied that we would get there soon.

Soon was not soon enough.

She died before we arrived.

We gathered around her bed with her husband and others. Someone played guitar and sang praise songs celebrating her resting place in Heaven. I was emotionally overcome to see the faith of this family and the people around them as I marveled at the power of music and faith during a very difficult time.

Noticing how the couple's faith had impacted the people in the hospital, I realized this was a clear example of spreading God's will "outside the walls of the church." They had an intimate walk with Jesus, a faith not of religiosity, but action.

God used our dear friend, even in her death, to deal with our hearts. Going through our trial of finances and relationship troubles, we felt we should have been more like this couple who lived their faith during the most trying time of their lives.

The experience strengthened our will, and reaffirmed our faith in God's plan for us.

As 2005 unfolded, we were still chipping away at the debt from 2004 and had no peace about what was coming next.

One pastor suggested we should shut down the festival. I tried to process and pray about his advice, but I didn't feel God was echoing his words.

Around that time, Vicki and I were invited on a trip to Israel with other pastors and their wives from around the United States—with all my expenses paid by the church I was attending at the time. I felt this Israel trip would be healing and direction for us, so we gratefully accepted.

Some people have said that for a Christian to travel to Israel and go to Jerusalem is like a Biblical scholar experiencing a year of seminary. I don't disagree. It was incredible to set foot in the land that once absorbed the footsteps of Jesus; walking along the coast of Galilee, you could almost envision Jesus calling His first followers and disciples, like visible echoes.

As Vicki and I soaked in everything, we were able to reflect and pray about God's direction for the future.

God's impact and presence was underscored when we visited with a Jewish shop owner who told us about the time a few years earlier when bombs were being targeted on Jerusalem. On that day the owner's wife felt a strong urge to close the shop an hour earlier than normal. Immediately after she locked up and walked away mortar shells hit the store. The couple showed me the marks still visible on part of the structure. The owners left the scars in the building to remind them that God was in control and His hand was leading them. A divine hand.

On our return from Israel, Vicki and I weren't sure how we were going to pay off the ministry's debts and if LifeLight would be leaving the fairgrounds or not, but we knew God wasn't calling us to cancel the festival.

Not long after we arrived home Luis Palau, whom we first met years before, called and said he was willing to come speak if our invitation was still open.

Of course, we said "yes."

Other than Billy Graham, Luis is one of the most respected evangelists over the last several decades. He has proclaimed the Gospel in festival settings all over the world to millions of people.

This was big for us and our small town—even if many in Sioux Falls were not familiar with his ministry.

Luis' call was followed by another; this time it was Pastor Mike Macintosh from San Diego, the former hippie who had become one of the more prominent Protestant leaders in America. He also wanted to speak at LifeLight.

These calls served as confirmation from above that we couldn't cancel LifeLight for one year—or any. They were also needed encouragement after we had parted ways with some good workers and people from our ministry.

These commitments, from a pair of Christian heavyweights, weren't the only good news we received. Faithful supporters came through to help with our finances. One businessman even gave us $20,000 to pay off the last of the debt. He said to consider it a loan, but later he changed it to a gift and asked God to bless the work we were doing.

Our finances were finally in order, but the resulting pain of questioning gossip and the lack of support from within our ranks was still stinging me.

Reflecting on the tumult of the past few months and my own life, I took a good look at my past experiences as a small business owner and thought, "Why didn't I rely on my business experience more?" Not to blame others for our mistakes, but the bad counsel we received was always "Wait. Wait. Wait… God will take care of it." God will, that was no lie, but you are always better off dealing with situations up front with communication than burying them and allowing problems to fester.

You are always better off dealing with situations up front with communication than burying them and allowing problems to fester.

Confrontation is not easy, but it's something we all need to push ourselves to do.

Even if it means confronting the fact that you have to find a new home for your massively successful music festival—with just a few months to spare.

■ ■ ■

Whether we verbalized it to anyone outside our own house or not, Vicki and I knew we needed to find a different home for the LifeLight festival.

Considering that our current home, the fairgrounds, barely contained our festival that was growing every year, the fact was hard to argue.

But it didn't seem like the thing to do when we were just a few months away from the start of the festival. And yet, once again, God sent us a message providing some clarity on the matter.

This time it came in the mail.

We had received a letter from the owners of a water park on the western outskirts of Sioux Falls some time before we really pondered the possibility of moving our festival in 2005. They wanted us to look at their location as a possible site for the festival. For whatever reason, I ignored the request, probably falling prey to the silly idea that water parks and Christian music don't mix.

Somehow the letter had made its way to the top of my mail pile, and I looked at the offer again. It had me thinking. "Let's take a drive out west and look at the water park," I suggested to Vicki.

Good thing we did.

Driving around the water park's expanded property lines of

160 acres, I saw the sprawling, slightly sloped hills of grass that engulfed the small cluster of water slides, tubing paths, and squirt gun stations. I could see how a fairly busy highway easily fed into the grasslands and fields that could serve as a parking lot. And I saw how a stage with hanging PA speakers and dual Jumbotron monitors could anchor a tiny valley that set like a natural amphitheater. Off to the side, I could picture how the area could collect a village of campers in a semi-tranquil setting that sat miles from the city limits.

Dipping back into my early visions of what LifeLight could be, I recognized some overlap with what was in front of me and started thinking, "This could work. Maybe we would finally get the grass sloping field we had envisioned?"

We were invited to a meeting with the owners who made the invite to host LifeLight on the Wild Water West property an official request. Christian music and water slides—it was sounding more and more like a fine combination. Our festival would get a new, sprawling home, and the water park would receive all the vendor rights to water and beverage sales during the event. Plus, they were excited about marketing our event and their water park together.

We presented the scenario to our board and, surprisingly, everyone was unified on the decision to move to Wild Water West. Even our good and faithful friend Pastor Kim, who was generally the most conservative on issues, told us moving was the right choice. That in itself was a confirmation we were making the right decision.

Next was telling the fair manager that we had decided to relocate. He took it graciously, but seemed confused about how this could work for us. He wasn't the only one.

Inside our ministry we were excited and fueled by the enthusiasm of a new vision. We held a luncheon the next day where we made the announcement to the local media—and received front page and nightly news coverage.

Yet with the plan out in the public, here came the naysayers again.

"You're moving to a water park?" was the standard reaction, paired with a sideways glance and nervous tilt, "How can that work?"

Some county officials wondered the same thing and then proceeded to tell us that even though the water park had a permit for large events, LifeLight did not, and we would have to apply for a separate zoning permit.

One of those public officials even said, "God might have told you to move, but you didn't consult with us." We were told that another county official had said, "I'll make it hard for them to move."

It was frustrating. The red tape and requirements felt more like power plays from people who wanted to have final approval on everything than the caution of officials truly concerned that our festival would be a traffic or noise nuisance for the "neighborhood."

Because of the gracious heart and passion of people who wanted to see this event continue, many rallied. A friend of the ministry, which had connections to experts from Minneapolis, even helped us. He was able to bring in a firm who had coordinated traffic for the Super Bowl. We carried letters of support from Senators, national radio groups, and media experts. The county sheriff spoke on our behalf, providing a voice of logic and common sense by reminding the county officials that they were making it easy for an event with a multi-million dollar impact on the community to decide to pick up and move to another, more accommodating city or county. The sheriff was well-spoken and to this day I am grateful for his help.

Still, the approval process made me realize that while we had the experience to facilitate such a large event, I had not developed the political relationships necessary for putting on a festival. So we went through all the appropriate meetings and procedures, which included plans for site development, traffic flow and counts, onsite parking, adequate onsite accommodations and lighting. Then, finally, with just 45 days before the start of the festival, we were given the green light to move ahead with our plans at Wild Water West. This looked impossible, and in most instances it would be. But the LifeLight crew has a habit of working together in a way that overcomes expectations. Even so, all the preparation time lines would need to fall into place perfectly.

To put this in perspective, putting on a festival for hundreds of thousands of people in prairie farm and grass lands mean we literally have to build a small city that can serve 300,000 people for four days. That means laying miles of electrical wire, lighting, and fencing; setting up generators and power sources; plotting camping and parking areas; establishing vendor areas; creating a "sewer system" by mapping out portable bathrooms and shower facilities for campers. Then, there's coordinating traffic flow plans, spraying for mosquitos, positioning the various stages so they don't bleed sound into each other, and the list goes on and on.

We needed a month of time just for a full crew to set up temporary fencing, mark out electrical paths, do the grading work for parking lots and traffic flow, and mow the grass on 160 acres. At times the timeline for this prep work felt impossible, but people grabbed hold of the vision and showed up by the hundreds to help us. Fortunately we had many longstanding and new volunteers. And, of course, some people were skeptical that we could get it all done.

As the festival approached, donations to our ministry began to drop. People were having a difficult time understanding what we saw in the isolated land around this water park. Some people even thought we were having the festival inside the water park, as if we'd want the musicians holding their electric guitars in a pool of water.

What we saw around the water park was potential. We envisioned a huge crowd gathered all over the grounds having fun with friends and family. We saw an event where people could build memories for years to come through the experience of the live music and festival activities drawing them closer with God.

One day, as the preparations were ongoing, I was riding around the property with a planner and a friend who was going to help with press and public relations. While sharing where things would go I could see some of the reservations on their faces. Their doubt wasn't dulled by the fact that during this tour, we even got stuck in a mud pit. It wasn't helping me prove my point of trusting the vision.

We saw an event where people could build memories for years to come through the experience of the live music and festival activities drawing them closer with God.

Despite the doubt, and the circumstances of refurbishing this land, our volunteer workload was making it all happen in the time frame we needed. Things were looking good. Maybe too good.

■ ■ ■

A few weeks before the festival was about to begin, a group was working and planning in the barn at my family's home base. We were preparing some festival supplies while my daughter and her friends practiced their rock music from a makeshift stage. I probably was showing off or maybe feeling energized by the music as I almost ran up a ladder to get to the platform above. I remember getting to the top when the ladder slid and fell to the floor under me. I reached with my right hand to grab a rafter, but that didn't work. I was falling.

My body slammed onto the ladder, which had just hit the concrete floor, and I landed on my right hip and leg. I wrenched in pain and then noticed my leg was positioned sideways, nearly at a right angle. As the music stopped, I remember hearing my daughter's scream.

This wasn't good.

The pain was setting in as I realized I could not move my leg or hip, which was protruding in an abnormal way. My mind was swirling with thoughts of what ifs, what needed to be done for the festival, and how I didn't have time for this inconvenience. Then the pain would spike, and all I could think was to pray for help. I kept praying for God to please rewind the last few minutes—to take away the pain, to ensure this accident wouldn't derail LifeLight. But I knew the reality of the situation was set, and that it was not good.

The paramedics arrived and moved me from the ground, to a stretcher, to the ambulance while they counseled me on the pain I was suffering and administered some drugs to dull it. As they began moving me, I started singing the songs of the Christian rock group Third Day who was scheduled to play at the upcoming festival. The paramedics said I sang all the way to the hospital—though I'm sure I was way off key.

My singing eventually stopped, but as they wheeled me into the operating room to repair my broken femur and crushed hip, I was still in festival prep mode. Before the doctors put me under for surgery, I looked at the surgeon and said, "You should consider being a financial sponsor for the festival."

I don't remember what he said, but the next thing I knew I was in a hospital room recovering. Suddenly, with the festival a few weeks away and the preparation as daunting as it ever had been, I was out of the picture for the first time since the very idea of LifeLight was sparked by that inner voice of divinity.

I spent a few days in the hospital and was lectured by the surgeon when I left for home. He said, "This was a very difficult surgery with rods, screws, and pins needed to hold your hip and femur in place. Don't screw it up. I need you sleeping in a recliner at night, and in fact, sitting for most of the time." He seemed quite nervous about me being on stage or hobbling around at LifeLight.

He asked if I was a runner. I said no, and he replied, "Good, I don't think you'll be one in the future. Use the crutches in moving around. This will be a longer recovery with lots of physical therapy to walk appropriately in the future."

Wow. That's just what a Type A guy in his 40s who bragged about hurdling fences and had a can-do attitude about everything wants to hear—especially with a festival approaching fast.

I was out of the picture for the first time since the very idea of LifeLight was sparked by that inner voice of divinity.

As we left the hospital we were faced with the burden of bills and the reality that I did not have health insurance to cover the accident. It just added to the stress that was already building in me about not being able to contribute to the festival that I started.

Some might say I'm a control freak; I prefer the term "control enthusiast." This festival set against grasslands and sloping hills was our dream. And as it was finally about to be realized, I was a temporary cripple, hobbling around on crutches while taking the required pain pills.

In a sense, it was terrifying for me not to have the festival conducted through me as it had been every year prior. But God gives us lessons in every day tragedies, and this was one for me. I had to believe the people we entrusted to construct and operate our dream were capable of getting the job done; or maybe, more accurately, allowing God's work to be directed through them.

So I relented, relaxed, and let Him take control.

As our volunteers appeared for help in every facet of the festival's construction, we felt that we just needed to stay out of God's way and let Him work. So often we, as humans, have to have our fingerprints all over everything we do, but God doesn't work that way. He says our battle is not against flesh and blood but a spiritual battle inside us.

Remember Ephesians 6, "For we do not wrestle against flesh and blood, but against the rulers, against the authorities, against the cosmic powers over this present darkness, against the spiritual forces of evil in the heavenly places."

It's a lesson worth remembering every day.

And, wouldn't you know it, when the festival's first day arrived everything was as it should be. We were ready for the 275,000 people who streamed into the grounds that year with the sun shining for the start of four days of music, messages, and a water park as well.

> People across generations, families, youth, and different culture groups all gathered in a non-threating environment to experience the love of God.

The festival-goers walked onto the grounds and finally saw

what we had seen in our minds for years: a sloping hill of alfalfa and grass filled with thousands of people glorifying God.

We could tell the festival-goers were excited and so were the water park owners who were praying for hot weather to compel people into their water park and to boost their water and soft drink sales.

After hearing all the doubts from people who failed to even try to see our vision of pairing LifeLight with a water park, we had a perfect fit. It was also an example of how to operate a contemporary Christian festival model that could be semi-mobile, yet bound to a particular region, as opposed to the days of stadium crusades that came through for a few days before leaving behind memories and inspiration.

We watched what we had prayed and dreamed for unfold before our eyes. People across generations, families, youth, and different culture groups all gathered in a non-threating environment to experience the love of God. There were plenty of church-going people who congregated for the music to celebrate their faith. But there was also a considerable chunk of those unchurched people who wandered in for the music and maybe even and maybe searching for hope.

Even our finances began to find balance through festival donations as people saw God work via His festival and His people. These people didn't just rally around us either. This was the year Hurricane Katrina devastated New Orleans just days before our festival. The LifeLight crowd responded with $28,000 in donations for the Katrina victims.

I stood back, the pads of my crutches snug under my armpits, watching everything unfold almost as if it was scripted from my dreams. The joy I felt is hard to describe. It was especially powerful as I watched and listened to Luis Palau address the crowd of attentive ears as he boldly presented the Gospel message as only he can with his wonderful blend of enthusiasm and hope.

It was inspiring in itself.

But what he said to me afterward was life—and LifeLight—changing.

He looked me in the eye and asked, "Why are you not speaking?"

I said, "Well, because we have you. And I'm hopping around on crutches and am on pain-killers. You never know what I might say at this point." He smiled and said, "No, I mean beyond this, normally. Why are you not speaking at the LifeLight festivals to the crowds?"

He wasn't just providing some polite compliments. Luis could see what I had been unable to, that I had to be more than just LifeLight's organizer and conduit. If there was a lesson to be found from the ill-timing of my injury, it was that LifeLight could be crafted without my hovering presence micro-managing what our team was doing. Luis recognized that these people around us couldn't provide the testimony that I could as the person who God spoke to about taking the church outside the walls.

"You have the passion for the lost that Jesus came for," he said. "Preach to the crowds here and wherever He leads."

He then looked at Julie, one of our board members and volunteers who had a full time job, and asked her, "Why are you not the festival director? Alan and Vicki need to be freed up to go and answer their personal calling in the ministry."

Here's a tip: when someone makes a statement and you feel God may be speaking through them, pay attention.

Luis' comments felt so affirming and encouraging that they couldn't be ignored.

It took a couple of years, but Julie did become the festival director and still holds that position with LifeLight today. And Vicki and I could change our roles to fulfill this calling.

Mike Macintosh also encouraged us to personally step further into the ministry. He said, "This is one of the greatest evangelistic outreaches I have ever been a part of." For Pastor Mike to say that was both inspiring and encouraging to us because he had a history of his own festivals, as well as a friendship and partnership with the Billy Graham family.

We were humbled by that statement because we knew it was God who was at work here; we simply listened to His wishes.

Mike was especially impressed with my daughter B.J.'s project and design for our New Life party, a special event for those who had just come to Christ.

> "This is one of the greatest evangelistic outreaches I have ever been a part of."

The New Life Party came about when Vicki said we needed to celebrate when someone's life was changed by accepting Christ; so Vicki asked (or maybe told), our 20-year-old daughter to design some New Life Party cards and plan on a birthday cake to celebrate spiritual birthdays at the festival.

Mike's daughter Sara, who was and is an extremely talented musician with a heart for people, agreed to sing in this New Life Party tent and pray with people. The party didn't attract the biggest crowd at the festival, but perhaps the plan was to minister to the few who really needed it.

I rode my golf cart over to the party and sat near the back of the tent as I heard my daughter say to the small group, "What happens after you accept Jesus matters. It's not just a heavenly head count; it's a constant, difficult, and beautiful work. And it's worth remembering. It is worth celebrating." There were some very personal stories told in that tent, and I got to witness God at work in my daughter and the celebrants as they shared stories about how Jesus had impacted their lives through LifeLight.

Then we all had cake.

After that party and the festival, I felt tired but refreshed.

It was so frustrating for me to watch the work happen around me during this festival, but the injury allowed me to step back and view how my family and our volunteers absorbed responsibilities and took the required tasks to a new level.

I was overjoyed to see God at work in such a powerful way, and without my fingerprints on it.

11

Mud Fest–The Year We Got a Little Dirty

We roared into 2006 with excitement and ambition, as the political game-playing around our new location and the internal gossip of the previous year fell behind us. We were committed to the Wild Water West property as our LifeLight site, and the ministry's finances were in a healthy state. But while these issues were finally settled, it didn't mean the year was going to be any less busy as we ventured into new territories and commitments.

Our missions work moved us to partner with Food for the Hungry, a Christian organization that aims to help end hunger wherever it strikes in the world. The battle took us to Ethiopia and Bangladesh.

Vicki's vision was to sponsor an entire village in Africa, which meant rallying people to the cause of contributing monthly to the physical, emotional, medical, and spiritual needs of the children in the village of Zeway, Ethiopia—the very people who God considers "the least of these" among us.

In total, over 2,000 children were sponsored through the LifeLight festival and outreaches, many of them orphans afflicted with AIDS. Over the past seven years, the LifeLight festival, through the generous support of our attendees, has helped raise close to $5 million for people in difficult situations.

Part of our travels that year in 2006 also took us to Bangladesh; the small country east of Southern India that's considered one of the worlds's most densely populated nations.

Driving is a little different in Bangladesh. The roads weren't so bad, except that there were no traffic signs or apparent rules. It was like being in a high-speed race with honking, swerving and cars crossing back and forth into each other's lanes. Rickshaws were everywhere and large busses passed each other so closely their sides sometimes scraped as they drove past. We were told many, many people die in the traffic.

The driving conditions weren't the only eye-opening sight. We were overwhelmed by the number of people; thousands upon thousands everywhere. There were people in the ditches, standing in storefronts, in the street, working in the streets, walking down the ditches, and on bicycles. There was a constantly churning sea of faces who we worried were lost. Less than one percent of the population of Bangladesh were believers in Christ. It seemed hopeless, despairing.

Where will they find hope? Who would tell them about Jesus?

The scene we were watching soon became even more real when we were dropped off at a muddy intersection near some rundown buildings. Here, a dark, young, thin man helped us onto the shabby bed of a rickshaw cart for the second leg of our transportation. He climbed on his rickety bicycle—one without a seat for him to rest on—and proceeded to pull us through the town, pedaling, pedaling, pedaling. Sweat poured down his thin frame and back. This was his job—every day, day in, and day out—and he probably worked for less than a dollar a day. The memory of this city is forever pressed into my mind. Where did they all lay their heads? Where will they find hope? Who would tell them about Jesus?

Their reality broke our hearts, as I am sure it breaks the heart of God.

Later, we were taken to a village in a remote area to visit a boy that my daughter Sarah had sponsored. His name is Roghu and he was 7 years old. His family lived in little block houses next to a sewage drainage line, and the stench was so strong it was difficult not react to the smell. But out of respect, we held back from covering our faces. Despite the odor, there was a beauty in the eyes of these people. Though we noticed how they were somewhat distant, which was odd since the people we usually approach in third world countries were so engaging that they often mobbed us upon arrival.

As we played games with Roghu and held him, the people started to really warm up to us. Eventually we were told Roghu and his family were considered by their society to be the "untouchables," the lowest level of the social caste system that are oppressed to the point that they can only get jobs as street sweepers or other labor-rich occupations that keep them away from the general public. They weren't used to being treated with an open, welcoming stance by people of a higher class.

Their reality broke our hearts, as I am sure it breaks the heart of God. In both the words of the Old and the New Testaments, Christ gives repeated strong warnings about how we should treat the poor among us. He even equates our ill treatment of them as personally offending Him. Through my travels, I have observed that He is found among the poor and oppressed of the world. And He calls us as followers to reach out to them as He esteems them highly in His Kingdom.

Once again we had served through an experience that changed us. Even the simple act of sharing a smile and a conversation with a person in crisis can change their countenance and give them a glimmer of hope. We continue to support Roghu to this day.

▪ ▪ ▪

These mission trips have an impact on the people we visit, but they hit close to home too. Our own children have been affected by mission work as they have observed Christian charity and had their own individual experiences with the Lord.

For instance, I remember watching with pride as my oldest daughter B.J. showed her heart during a mission trip to Mexico. She was leaving the trip early because of some previous obligations, so we took her to the El Paso airport. We arrived at the airport and were unloading her gear from the vehicle when, suddenly, we couldn't find her. We looked around and saw her talking to a homeless man, saying she wouldn't give him money but would buy him a meal. B.J. was asking questions and ministering to him. I thought to myself, "This is real ministry, and it is the Lord working in and through her."

My daughters have always joined us on mission trips and they have spread the message of the Lord in their lives—sharing the Gospel is a central part of their lives.

As a father their actions make me feel proud but also quite relieved. Chasing the dream to realize LifeLight meant I had to sacrifice a lot of time with my family so I could be involved in the ministry. When I see our children take on the message of faith for themselves it is a joy to watch.

"I have no greater joy than to hear that my children are walking in Truth." 3 John 1:4

■ ■ ■

The festival of 2006 was, of course, not incident free.

In the build-up of doubt and apprehension after our announcement the previous year that the festival would be moving to the Wild Water West grounds, many people warned us that site could be problematic if there was a major rain storm. The land was low and had no real drainage system in place. That wasn't an issue in our first year at the water park, but on the opening night of the 2006 festival, the rain started and didn't stop.

Our festival site was dotted with puddles of water that were nearly everywhere. And where there wasn't a puddle, there was mud. We used plywood and cardboard wherever we could to make walking paths, but there were more people at the festival than our makeshift trails could handle, so many of the festival-goers were traipsing through the water and mud. They got wet and messy and lost quite a number of shoes that were sucked down into the goop… when the land dried after the festival that fall, the land owners were finding hundreds of shoes for weeks. As you can imagine, this also meant that all kinds of cars, trailers, and campers were stuck in the mud. It was a logistical nightmare.

The rain continued to the point that, as Evangelical leader and famed author Rick Warren spoke from the main stage to a wet crowd, a group of us huddled backstage contemplating canceling the remaining days of the festival.

It seemed the critics may have been right, I thought to myself, "At this rate this festival is going to be under water if it doesn't stop raining." And yet as we looked out from the stage to the incoming road, cars were lined-up, still coming toward the wet grounds.

Meanwhile, many of the festival-goers were having fun in the mud, sliding down muddy hills that used to be lush with green grass. The conditions would not stop the young people from having their party.

As they frolicked, making the best out of a messy situation, we wrestled over the gravity of cancelling the rest of the festival. Financially, it would be a big loss. We would still have to pay all the bands and production units while taking away two days of fundraising through the festival. Then there would be the consequences of public perception—that this festival site was flawed or that people might not want to travel long distances to come to a festival that could be cancelled by a heavy rainstorm.

We regrouped after the last concert in the pouring rain of that Friday night and agreed to decide the festival's fate the next morning, which had more rain in the forecast. And we prayed.

By the next morning the heavy rain had stopped, so the festival could continue. But even though the moisture wasn't falling from the sky, it was still soaked into grounds supporting the stages, the vendors, and the thousands and thousands of people ready for a day of music and message.

Before we could restart the festivities, we had to reinforce some of the infrastructure.

We put the word out through our local media, including the area Christian radio station Life 96.5, that we were going to open up the second day and proceed as planned, but would need lots of help to get the grounds ready. That regional radio station grew with us in partnership through many years with a common thread of reaching out with the Good News. This year especially, we would be so very thankful for the relationship. Once again God's will came through as many people rallied around us to provide aid. Some showed up with heavy equipment like skid-steer loaders, pay-loaders, and tractors to move water and dirt to prevent flooding. Others brought truckloads of wood chips to provide a drier base for the flocks of people to stand on. Through this help, the festival not only continued through a semi-wet Saturday, but Sunday's weather was finally pleasant. The decision to persist was the right one.

I watched that Sunday morning as a worker in an orange shirt, signifying he was an inmate from the county jail who had been allowed to help us under supervision, was moving mud and reinstalling the barrier fence. He paused as speaker Joe White gave the invitation for people to pray. The worker turned toward the stage and tears began to stream down his face. He looked toward heaven and then bowed his head in prayer. Tears rolled down my face as well, while I looked toward heaven and said, "Yes, Lord, forgive me for my doubt. This is what LifeLight is all about, if even for the one. You died for the one. It's all worth it."

12

Here and There

It's the same all over the world. Whether as part of a large crowd listening to Christian rock bands or surviving in a small, impoverished village that felt like a place Jesus might have actually visited—people want to hear the Good News of Jesus in a relevant way.

That latter example is exactly what happened in the fall of 2007 while we led a mission trip to Ethiopia's western territories to meet with the pastors and people of the tiny village called Belo. In truth, it almost felt like the ends of the earth—an arid region where the roads are nothing more than dirt and the people live under thatch roof huts. Electricity is scarce in Belo, as is clean water and consistent food sources. In other words, it's a far cry from the many amenities found at a music festival.

We were there on a mission to visit children sponsored at

LifeLight events and to simply tell them that God loves them, to tell them they are not forgotten, and that they could have a relationship with God, the Creator of the universe, through a relationship with Jesus. This is the commandment that we were given in the Bible—to go and tell others about Jesus. We brought birthing kits, hygiene packets, school necessities, and medical supplies that were desperately needed in this part of the world. A visit and word of encouragement was many times what was really wanted.

While meeting and speaking with the Belo residents, we were moved by their intense hunger for the Gospel. We were compelled to present a movie night in the middle of the village square showing the Campus Crusade for Christ film "Jesus" in their native Amharic language. Our movie screen was a tarp strung up between two poles. Our projector was powered by a generator. As we walked the crowd prior to the start of the movie the gathering of people exuded an electric energy.

As the movie set in the time of Jesus' life on Earth played, it seemed to echo the scenery around our makeshift theater. It was almost as if we were transported into the movie itself.

Cattle lowing by the manger was never more real than in the smells and sounds of that scene. Behind the crowd of movie-goers chickens pecked the bared ground between the hooves of laden donkeys in the market. Sheep were moving about our midst as the movie played.

An oxen-pulled wagon even stopped its progression through town so the driver could climb onto the back of his wagon to watch the movie.

By the time the film concluded the crowd had swelled and one of the local pastors gave the audience an opportunity to respond to the movie and invite Christ into their lives. The response was overwhelming as many people asked for prayer, while others just needed to talk and share their burdens with someone.

It felt as though we had opened the Bible to the book of Acts and walked right into its story setting.

As we packed up and headed back to our little compound rain began to pour down on us as if the heavens had just opened with showers of blessings. Dr. Jim, who was part of our team, looked at me with a smile and said, “Oh God, now you’re just showing off. What timing!” God showed up in Belo, Ethiopia, and there was spiritual work taking place; we just needed to be there in obedience to His calling.

The Spirit of God was there in that small village, just as He was when hundreds of thousands of His people came together.

Even though it seemed we were visiting a place lost in time, those gatherings in Belo carried a small glimpse of the energy, excitement, and enthusiasm of a LifeLight festival. The Spirit of God was there in that small village, just as He was when hundreds of thousands of His people came together.

▪ ▪ ▪

This trip to Ethiopia was especially meaningful to us as our team was a small, intimate group of nine people comprised of Vicki & I, our middle daughter Sarah, and six other special people God sent us. One of the team members was Sarah Buller, a devoted, passionate young teenager who was abandoned to God. She was excited to be going on a mission trip to Africa, a place her father had told her about from his previous visit. Even though she was younger than the age limit we normally allowed to come without their parents, we agreed to let Sarah become part of the group because she was wise beyond her years, and we were so impressed with her family.

She bunked with our own daughter, Sarah, and brought a whole level of excitement along for our journey as she wanted to experience everything the trip had to offer and lived every day as if it were her last—with a smile and joy.

Little did we know that her life would be cut short (in earthly eyes). Just two years later Sarah was in a car accident while she was serving the Lord she loved on a mission trip in South Africa. Sarah had spent her life on the family farm in rural Minnesota, but her passion was to attend any youth event she could be a part of. The LifeLight festival was one of her many adventures and she always brought as many friends as she could. Her love for the Lord was contagious. Meeting young people like Sarah gives me hope for the next generation.

She made such an impact on us and all the people of our ministry that LifeLight set up a scholarship fund for mission trips in her name—the Sarah Buller Scholarship Fund. Sarah had touched so many lives in her short years and her memorial scholarship continues that legacy by touching lives that she has never even met. Sarah's passion for missions fueled our decision that the fund's main purpose is to give seeking, young people the opportunity to be able to experience overseas mission outreach. Over and over again, the legacy of Sarah encourages young people into missions. Each year free trips are awarded to winning applicants for their travel with LifeLight to another country to share the Good News and to experience what made Sarah live so passionately.

We may never know the impact of Sarah's life until we reach eternity.

Sarah's death was also a reminder to Vicki and I about how short life is and renewed the urgency in us of sharing the Good News of the Gospel of Jesus Christ and His hope for today and tomorrow.

■ ■ ■

Later in 2007 I experienced another awakening as I felt the Lord had some things for me to say.

I had spent a lifetime in sales and building my business to provide for my family and to allow me to start the LifeLight ministry. It had been five years since I committed myself to full time ministry, and the passion within my heart was compelling me to speak about God with the same passion and enthusiasm that I spent running a business—actually, there was more passion.

Every once in a while, a quote from a movie pops out at me and encapsulates what I'm going through. The 1981 film "Chariots of Fire" was one such movie, especially when Olympic runner Eric Liddel says, "When I run, I feel His pleasure." Much like Liddel, I felt God's presence when I was preaching or talking about Him. It increasingly felt like it was time for me to do more of the speaking and spend less time hiding behind the administrative duties of the LifeLight ministry.

God wanted me to do more than facilitate an annual music festival. He had brought people around us to enable me to start letting go of some of the festival duties. When I was in Africa speaking to the pastors or motivating a child sponsorship organization I felt God's pleasure and my calling. The adjustments took time, but God was putting things in place for me to be more relational than task-oriented.

This has been harder than I thought to accomplish however, releasing things to others allowed us to be available to do whatever God put in front of us. We found joy in visiting with people that are launching their own ministries, encouraging young evangelists and imputing passion in their lives, and speaking at any opportunity we had to share the claims of Jesus.

The greatest joy has come in being able to preach and teach, especially in third world countries such as Haiti, Ethiopia, Mexico, and Pakistan, to people who are so transparent about their need for God. The quest is to go both here and there as God opens doors.

It works because a group of ordinary people said, yes to God's calling to carry the life-changing message of Jesus Christ from the pews to the streets, whether those streets were in their hometown or halfway across the world.

Over the years LifeLight has gone through many changes and is still run in large part through the dedicated help of volunteers, our warriors for the Kingdom. The quality that stands out most to me about our volunteers is that they are all serving out of a calling rather than just filling in spot for a job.

Yes, we are still a small ministry; yet, we have been involved in the extraordinary work of God. It works because a group of ordinary people said, yes to God's calling to carry the life-changing message of Jesus Christ from the pews to the streets, whether those streets were in their hometown or halfway across the world.

■ ■ ■

During my various speaking engagements, or even casual conversations with random people, I'm often asked if this "festival thing" is actually a way to reach the un-churched people or if it's just a big party for Christians. As our friend Pastor Clyde once said, "So what if it were a party for Christians? I know of nothing that motivates and reignites that faith of the local church more than the festival. It raises the standards for worship bands, seminars, and fellowship within the body of Christ ... what an honor to have this event in our city."

It's nice to have level-headed, supportive guys like Clyde on our side.

And, yes, sometimes LifeLight does feel like a big party for Christians.

Like seeing 70,000 or more people singing along to the smooth sounds of worship singer Chris Tomlin as they point their waving hands skyward under a bright, clear September moon.

Or walking through the mosaic of quilts and lawn blankets laid over a grassy slope to hear various people—likely strangers—sharing Bible passages or simply remarking on how refreshing it is for them to mix their faith and their leisure time in a peaceful setting.

But the festival is so much more as the secular world joins us, many of them coming to meet the One we are celebrating. And there's a lot to celebrate inside our annual festival. The problem with this "party" is the same problem with most parties; it has to end.

But the festival is so much more as the secular world joins us, many of them coming to meet the One we are celebrating.

After three days of reinforcing their spiritual base among the like-minded, these people have to go home, sometimes to walk the path of faith by themselves.

That's one reason why shortly after the festival ends each year, we're slammed with simple messages that say things like, "We can't wait until LifeLight next year!" Most of these are sent by teens and adolescents. After a while, we began thinking, "They shouldn't have to wait until next year. We should go to them!" So we did.

In 2005 we began regional LifeLight tours featuring a handful of the worship and rock bands that played the festival each year. With this outreach, we weren't looking to book arenas and auditoriums in metropolitan cities. We wanted to take it to the smaller cities that are often overlooked by tour promoters. Our objective was clear: we were taking music and the hope of Jesus to the overlooked and forgotten. And we knew that lives were going to change. We wanted mainly to focus our ministry on the youth, much in the same way the LifeLight festival started, by drawing them with music that appeals to their tastes. But our festivals and tours have shown us time and time again that we shouldn't stereotype our audience.

During one of these tour stops in a small Nebraska town, the scene was typical—the bands were rocking and the music was loud, bouncing off the walls of the local gymnasium like ricochets of sound. The kids were also bouncing along to the beat of rock band VOTA. Bryan, the lead singer, had the crowd captivated and was compelling the kids to sing along and lose themselves to the music. I was standing off stage, the sounds pounding on my chest like a dull jackhammer. I had just spoken and given the crowd a chance to have prayer or receive a Gospel booklet. Many of the kids wanted to talk or at least say thanks after the concert, so I stayed around afterward as the stage was being torn down. That's when I saw something out of place—a little 80-year-old lady was still sitting near the back. Some people relayed the message that she wanted to meet me. As I walked across the gym in her direction I could only imagine what she would say, and what I was picturing was not very good. Typically we were scolded about our loud music in situations similar to this. But, instead, she told me that when I had spoken earlier she had committed her life to Christ.

I was shocked, in a good way.

I asked her thoughts on the rock music, and she said, "Oh, I kind of enjoyed it."

Like Pastor Clyde, she saw the greater picture beyond the sight of the "party." She said the youth in her town needed this, but it was the message and the words of Christ that had moved her to come to the Savior in a real way for the first time in her 80 years. She then said how much the music and lyrics of VOTA had meant to her. Right before playing the song "You Alone," which Bryan dedicated to his late grandmother, he told the crowd about how he got to share the Good News of Christ with his grandmother before she passed away and how she had told him about that song ministering to her. That testimony resonated with my new 80-year-old friend, and just hearing her describe the impact it had on her was powerful.

I imagine she had been in churches throughout her life, and yet it took a Christian rock concert for this 80-year-old woman to migrate her relationship with Christ from her head to her heart.

I imagine she had been in churches throughout her life, and yet it took a Christian rock concert for this 80-year-old woman to migrate her relationship with Christ from her head to her heart.

13

Moving Miracles

Our 2008 journey began somewhere we had already been as we reflected on the physical places where this ministry started—specifically, in a file cabinet that sat next to the dining table in our family home. This is where the early LifeLight business was conducted, stored, and organized.

As LifeLight grew, so did the contents of this cabinet. Eventually we had to move its contents to our home office where Vicki stored the homeschooling supplies. For years this office was where we coordinated band confirmations for our festival lineups, took the calls of people hoping to speak at our gatherings, and organized the technical backend which allowed the festival to have light, food, and a campground. And, just to be clear here, calling it an office might give you the wrong idea of where this room was held.

The "office" was part of a rough metal pole barn that housed my daughters' horses alongside some random cats, opportunistic swallows, and maybe an owl. Though it might sound romantic working next to the animals, try talking to some booking agents while a horse whinnies in the background.

We later moved the office to a small bungalow on our property, but as the ministry continued to grow, it was an inconvenient location that wasn't quite up to code.

Eventually, we had to move. For a couple of years we were able to get rental space in a nice building where we could conduct LifeLight business across the hall from a Christian coffee house that gave a stage to a variety of musicians from rock to Gospel to hip-hop.

Though it might sound romantic working next to the animals, try talking to some booking agents while a horse whinnies in the background.

It was a nice change of scenery. Still, not everything was perfect in this new home.

With our increased staffing, we weren't just sharing office rooms, we were sharing cubicles and playing musical desk space—moving to an open computer whenever somebody left the office for an appointment or a lunch break. Once again, we needed to move.

So in the fall of 2007 we began touring rental office spaces all over town, but everything was out of our price range…which was just north of nothing. The possibility of finding a new work home appeared dismal, but we prayed on the situation and searched in faith.

During this time the landlords of our office, Rick and Sonja, heard about our search for a better space and told us about a building they had recently purchased to use as commercial rental property. One fall day Rick and his son, who was a realtor, took us through the building, but as I walked the halls I was wondering why we were there. They knew what we paid for rent. They had to know we could not afford this spot. So I asked what they had in mind, and they suggested we could take the lower floor of the split-level property, and they could rent out the top floor. It was a good idea, but still not a financially feasible one for our ministry. Besides, if we could rent the building, we would need it all.

We thanked them for the offer, but it wasn't going to work. Before we parted, Rick and his son asked if we would pray about it, which we did. We then left to lead our mission trip to Ethiopia.

After returning from Africa we met with Rick and Sonja to discuss the building again. They had been praying as well and they said they thought we were supposed to have the building, though they couldn't just give it to us. They said they would sell it to us for $100,000 less than its appraised value.

We were grateful for the offer, but, again, we didn't have the money and were not confident that a bank would loan it to us. We prayed and waited. We also sent a letter to a few faithful donors who had indicated that they may be willing to help if we found a building.

During the wait our board advised that this probably wasn't the best time to secure a new property for the ministry. We were slowly accepting that we would have to give up hope of landing this building, but we had to visit it one last time as we began to feel what Rick and Sonja felt—this building could be the right place for us. During that walk-through our team prayed inside the property's break room, asking God to reveal His plan for us as we did not believe LifeLight should have a formal fundraising campaign.

We later found out that at the same time we were gathered to pray inside that building, a friend of the ministry was across the street from that very property. She knew about our situation and prayed about this location being a good fit for the LifeLight headquarters. It wasn't long after that she and her husband handed us a check for $250,000.

It was a gift from God. Even though it was not enough to purchase the building, a few other faithful friends of the ministry pulled together more funds. At the end of December we bought the building with an 80 percent down payment.

God's divine hand once again led us toward a dream realized.

God's divine hand once again led us toward a dream realized. It was a beautiful Christmas gift.

■ ■ ■

We have all types of musical genres at the LifeLight festival—from rap and hip-hop, to rock and country Gospel. The variety helps us fulfill our mission of attracting people from all walks of life to this free gathering that hopes to entertain while its sends people toward salvation. But, the Souled Out stage is a different animal in itself.

This is the place where the people with tattoos and facial piercings flock to hear the kind of hard rock or heavy metal sounds that are built around distorted guitar riffs and possibly some screaming vocals, much like the coarse voice of Sesame Street's Cookie Monster. It all depends on your pop culture perspective.

A pastor once told me, "Thank you for keeping that stage a long way from the Gospel stage so my people won't have to walk past it."

He was kidding, but the Souled Out stage can be rather uncomfortable for some people who dare not tread past convention.

While the musical motif may seem like a paradox to the people who grew up listening to the Bill Gaither family singing traditional, safe Gospel songs, this blast of "noise" and aggression can be an effective way to attract the young, un-churched masses that we started this festival to help. Think of it similar to the way a missionary learns the language of the people he is trying to reach.

That was never more evident than in 2008 when the Souled Out stage became the scene of an unexpected awakening.

That year the stage featured Seventh Day Slumber, a hard rock act that wasn't too abrasive—lead singer Joseph Rojas sang as much as he screamed. Joseph and I were speaking before they played and I encouraged him to share his personal story from the stage. So he did, addressing the crowd of mostly teen and adolescent rock fans about his past life abusing drugs and alcohol and his attempted suicide that was only thwarted by the fast action of an ambulance crew. The victim of a tough upbringing, Joseph was perhaps on his way toward another suicide attempt, but he found hope after surrendering his life to Jesus.

That was never more evident than in 2008 when the Souled Out stage became the scene of an unexpected awakening.

I'd heard Joseph's story before and it was very moving. But that night, late into the darkness of a summer evening, I was standing from a different viewpoint at the main stage where Michael W. Smith was finishing a set of his piano-driven worship songs in front of a crowd of tens of thousands of people. When Michael finished, I was to follow, speaking about the love and grace of Christ to the audience of our more mainstream festival-goers, the type of people who mostly look and act like you'd see them sitting in church every Sunday morning.

But back at the Souled Out stage, Joseph shared his story and then asked everyone in his crowd who had ever contemplated suicide to raise their hands. Hundreds of hands pointed in the air. He then asked who had thought about suicide in the last month. A number of hands went down, but plenty remained. "Last week?" Hands remained hanging upward. Then Joseph paused, and as his voice quivered a bit and he said, "Is there anyone here tonight who has considered suicide maybe even today, and maybe you wouldn't be with us now if it weren't for the fact that you're here at this concert, at this festival, right now?"

There were still hands held up against the night sky.

There were still hands held up against the night sky.

Joseph then asked the crowd to back up and make some room in front of the stage. Now, if you're familiar with rock concert tendencies, this is not an easy request. The kids pack themselves against the barrier in front of the stage with near hydraulic force. Yet, within seconds, the crowd had moved itself about 30 yards back from the stage.

Joseph responded by asking anyone there who wanted real change, real hope, to come forward to the stage on the count of three.

"One. Two." He paused for effect before yelling, "Three!"

At the same moment, I was just about to go on the main stage for my speaking assignment when my phone began buzzing. It was Tony, our festival head of operations. He never called my cell phone during the festival as we mostly used two-way radios to relate festival issues and business. So all the red flags went up when I saw him calling me on the phone. I was nervous as I answered it, worrying we'd experienced a power outage or collapsed stage with resulting injuries.

"Dude, you won't believe what just happened," he said. "They ran, man. They ran."

When Joseph hit three hundreds of people fought through the crowd and sprinted toward the front of the stage, dropping to their knees as they wept and asked for the help of Jesus. Prayer responders flooded to the Souled Out area to help with the masses but were overwhelmed by the need for prayer.

I swallowed the lump in my throat and thought, "Thank you God," and then, "If only the crowd in front of this stage would be so transparent about their lives now."

This is what LifeLight is all about. It's why we work through the thousands of hours of labor, paper work, and contract negotiations. It's why we withstand sunburns, sleep deprivation, and missed meals in the quest to keep the festival running. Though we can get caught up in the glamour of backstage elbow-rubbing with musical celebrities or the ego-stroking of radio and newspaper interviews, the reason some of us are on stage in front of tens of thousands of people is to experience God saving souls.

"Dude, you won't believe what just happened," he said. "They ran, man. They ran."

Humbled by the moment I prayed, "Give me the words as I prepare to talk to this crowd, and thank you for reaching and literally rescuing all those young people." The words that followed were pretty obvious. I told this congregation about what had just happened in front of the Souled Out stage, and followed Joseph's example. A few minutes later, thousands of people at the main stage began their own journeys with God, by simply saying, "yes" to Him.

I'll never forget that night. I'm sure all those people who gave their lives to God that evening won't either.

■ ■ ■

The high of the 2008 festival had us floating for months. But another epic low crashed into our life.

Well, actually, it crashed a lot of people's lives.

Later that fall, just weeks before a Presidential election, the stock market crashed on Wall Street and set off a financial quake that sunk us into a recession.

> Turns out, God wasn't ready to see LifeLight go dim.

This was bad for much of America as scores and scores of people who had worked decades to accrue retirement funds saw their investments shrink. Others lost their jobs as various corporations responded to the grim financial forecast with layoffs or staff reductions. In the non-profit realm, where we exist, the donations we rely on to support our work and workers were drying up like a slug on pavement during a 100 degree day. People were just trying to pay their own bills, much less the expenses of ministries like ours.

I remember being in my office alone, wondering if we were done again. It seemed like we had been in this situation before. We were sitting in uncertainty about our sustainability as we carried on our only plan of believing that God would lead us toward what we needed to survive as we did His work.

Every time we were in need of money, volunteers, property, or simply hope, God had provided us with what was necessary.

But things felt different this time. We needed $500,000 by January just to pay our expenses.

I sat in my office worrying about our situation and my phone rang. It was a friend who had been in my shoes before, and his counsel was to at least prepare for who we might have to let go and how we might cut the ministry expenses to continue. He prayed for me. The phone call affirmed to us that we weren't walking this path alone; I was encouraged, yet the reality still confronted us.

When the phone call ended Vicki and I prayed too. With just six weeks to go before our payments were due, a hopeful outcome didn't seem possible. Then we relayed the news of our deficit to the community and our donors. The media even helped get the message out, which was humbling since we were just one of many ministries in such a scenario.

As the time ticked through the holidays and past the New Year, we still believed God was not done with the LifeLight festival and our satellite ministries. People gave from their hearts with small and large gifts that were all received with the sincerest gratitude. Yet, as 2009 began, we were still short of our goal and wondering if, after 11 years and a myriad of uncertain moments about our futures, LifeLight was finally coming to an end—or at least a hiatus.

Turns out, God wasn't ready to see LifeLight go dim. By January 4th, we received over $500,000. This amount was enough to cover all of our remaining festival expenses and payroll allowing us to move forward—Praise God! For our small ministry it was truly a miraculous sign of encouragement that we were doing the right thing—His plan. During a period of grave economic despair, it was also a realization that our ministry was being embraced by the very community that we pledged to help.

During a period of grave economic despair, it was also a realization that our ministry was being embraced by the very community that we pledged to help.

14

Riding the Wave of Change, Again

"This is our last year here at the water park."

Those words finally came out of my mouth three months before the 2009 festival. I stood in front of a hastily-put-together press conference to break the news that, like Greek philosopher Heraclitus' believed, the only constant in LifeLight was change.

The responses were predictable: "Are you serious?"

I was.

"But it's just getting to the place where we are comfortable. We have put a lot into the grounds here."

That was the point, I told them. Though this location west of Sioux Falls provided further realization to the dream I had years and years earlier, the vision was for a place in which we could grow. A permanent place.

We had a great five-year run at the water park and were

grateful to the owners for the opportunity that allowed the festival to finally be staged in a natural setting. But it was their land and business to run. As we continued putting money and development into their grounds, we knew that we were approaching a time when our needs could conflict with the park's plans for expansion. We also had a ministry to operate and an expectation to be good stewards with God's money, which was being used to rent the location.

And, in typical LifeLight fashion, we didn't have a replacement location selected. We didn't even have a few possibilities. We just knew the time was right for a change.

As we pondered what was next, a local pastor who had been a great help to us over the years came into Vicki's office and started talking about what was going on in his life. His unexpected visit was only days before the festival, so Vicki was trying to pack up various things to take to the grounds and still at least seem to be politely attentive while only half listening. But when he said, "This is the scripture I am teaching on…" she paused her rushed packing and opened her Bible to the passage, Numbers 14:8 "... And they spoke to all the congregation of the sons of Israel, saying, 'The land which we passed through to spy out is an exceedingly good land. If the Lord is pleased with us, then He will bring us into this land and give it to us—a land which flows with milk and honey.'"

The pastor, who hadn't been told of our plans to relocate, said he didn't know how relevant his sermon scripture was, but maybe it was meant for us. Vicki found me later to tell me what had happened and said, "God is going to give us the land!" She highlighted for me the part of scripture that said, "He will bring us into the land and give it to us." This was confirmation of what we felt God had already said to us.

I believed because God had provided for us so many times in

the past that it was difficult to discount this suggestion. But in the weeks after the festival had ended, it became harder to hold onto hope of free land because the reality of the festival being homeless was getting closer and closer every day. Even if the promise from scripture Vicki was holding on to were to come true on its own, our human nature got in the way. We began searching for property.

We formed a local ad-hoc task force made up of business leaders and government officials who were gracious enough to meet with us and brainstorm places that could accommodate the hundreds of thousands of people whom the festival attracted. It was easy to sense that many of these people on the task force thought we were foolish to give up on the water park without a replacement selected.

"... And they spoke to all the congregation of the sons of Israel, saying, 'The land which we passed through to spy out is an exceedingly good land. If the Lord is pleased with us, then He will bring us into this land and give it to us—a land which flows with milk and honey.'"

One of the members told me, "You know, if my son quit his job without having another lined-up, I would tell him it's not wise." Point taken, but that's not how God was having us step out in trusting Him. It's hard to explain this kind of out-of-the-box faith, which has its ups and downs. Ultimately, when you have seen God provide so many times, and you realize it is His ministry, you learn to let go of those controlling instincts and follow His lead. The outcome is a rush well beyond any successes we ever achieve through our own planning.

Still, we felt we had to plan for a more realistic solution.

One official said we could try and come together and build an event grounds over a seven-year plan. Vicki told them, "With all due respect, in seven years the Lord might even have come back. We won't be waiting around seven years to study and plan without action."

Another common suggestion was to renegotiate and stay at least another year at Water Wild West so we had time to find the right site. This was completely rational; yet, we felt the door had been closed, and God was not giving us a peace about staying there. Could we have misheard God? Maybe. But we sensed He was at work and that we were to be faithful.

We called a press conference to announce our plans to the public. A reporter asked, "You mean you are moving, and you don't know where you are going? Do you have a reserve fund for purchasing land? Are you doing a capital fund drive?" Our response was, "God will provide. He knows where we are going and perhaps someone is sitting on 200 acres of farm land and wants it to be used for God's purposes."

"You think someone is going to give you the land?" another reporter asked.

I said, "We believe that there is someone willing to offer us the land for free for the LifeLight festival, and God will lead them to that decision."

That statement confounded the business and worldly model of thinking and made for interesting media stories. But we were still waiting for some sign of land being delivered to us.

As we waited, other cities in the region contacted us saying they understood the economic and spiritual benefits of hosting our festival in their city limits. These locations in Mitchell and Yankton, South Dakota, were very compelling and were offered to us for free. But we weren't settled about the idea of moving the largest Christian music festival in the country out of the Sioux

Falls metropolitan area.

Some of our supporters questioned our decision to spurn those offers, which was to be expected. Many people like the security of certainty. We felt confident God would provide again; but His methods continue to amaze us.

▪ ▪ ▪

One day shortly after the press conference, we received a phone call from Karla Lems. I didn't know the family but their name had been dropped by a number of people in our Christian circle which led me to call and leave a phone message a few weeks earlier. I remember Karla's voice on the phone as she told me she understood we were looking for land and asked us to take a drive with her and her husband Gaylon around Lincoln County, which covers the southern side of Sioux Falls and the area underneath it along Interstate 29.

With Karla and Gaylon as our tour guides, we looked at a number of locations that had been used as farmland and then stopped for coffee at the Pederson farmstead. Evelyn Pederson, Karla's recently widowed mother, visited with us and then asked, "Would you consider having the festival here on the land around the farm? There would be over 200 acres available to you."

Vicki and I looked at each other with excitement and a bit of nervousness, as if there was a caveat attached.

Then she added, "Oh, it would be free, and you could have it as a permanent home."

The Pedersons offered a free, 40-year lease that automatically renews for another 40 years. This family had farmed for decades and leased out lots of land for farming; yet, after the passing of Dwayne Pederson, they had been praying and discussing what to do with the farming operation. They really saw it as a blessing to give land to be used to harvest people in place of the corn they had grown for decades. They had attended the LifeLight festival in the past and understood the need to reach people outside the walls of the church.

The only stipulation from Evelyn was that ministry would take place on the land, meaning that the property would only be used for Christian purposes and not for secular concerts devoid of His Good News. This was not a difficult stipulation for us.

The offer left us in awe—both of their generosity and the awesome hand of a loving God. Words could not express how we felt leaving their home that day or how we feel still to this very day. The Pederson family has continued to bless LifeLight with their generosity many times over by allowing us to use their buildings, donating harvest money to the ministry, and upgrading the property. And, to top it all off, Evelyn often bakes us homemade goodies to make it feel like we're "home."

Perhaps one of the best confirmations that this was the right place for LifeLight came just before we left that meeting. Vicki asked if they ever had cows or bees on the land. The family confirmed that in the past they had a beekeeper, and though they hadn't had dairy cattle in many years, the dairy barn was still a stone's throw from the house. Milk and honey; the scripture fit—this was home.

"Well, you can use it 'til Jesus comes back."

Evelyn ended the meeting by saying, "Well, you can use it 'til Jesus comes back."

As of this printing, we're still at the farm.

15

Global Vision and a Place called Home

There was a renewed excitement and passion that came with finally having LifeLight bound to a permanent home. It provided a new sense of purpose as more dreams and visions unfolded for the future of the festival, as well as the ministry as a whole.

Yet, the doubters arrived as we moved into this new location, just as their choruses of apprehension and scrutiny had serenaded us toward our shifts to the fairgrounds and Wild Water West years before.

"Well, that's a great piece of ground they got for a festival, but not for 2010. It takes much longer than the time they have to get that land ready for a massive festival."

These critics harped we wouldn't be able to use the property for our festival until the next year.

"You won't be able to get grass even planted there. It's a corn field, and there is still snow on the ground."

Well, they were right about a couple things. There was still snow on the ground that spring of 2010, and it had been a very wet year marked by heavy snow that stayed later than usual and an abundance of spring rain. Very few farmers could even get into the fields to plant. But, Dwayne, the land's owner who had farmed this ground all his life, had installed drain tiles in some of his fields years earlier so he could get into them quicker for planting and harvesting. His foresight became a blessing to us as we planted grass in April and watched it grow while other farmers in the area were unable to get into the fields. It felt to us that the Lord was handling everything for us.

The fields where corn was harvested before were now being prepared to harvest souls.

The fields where corn was harvested before were now being prepared to harvest souls. Wouldn't it be wonderful if Dwayne was looking down from heaven somehow and seeing the Lord's work on this land he poured his heart into for so many years?

The 2010 festival on Pederson's land was amazing as we watched 320,000 people from all over the nation and world descend upon this farm in rural South Dakota for our music festival.

It was a rather bizarre sight, seeing scores of young music fans dressed in black T-shirts or vibrant, colorful tank tops weaving through an area of food and merchandise vendors positioned beside a row of towering metal grain bins—the stereotypical clash of city kids and farm life melding together in front of us. Not far away, cars parked in fields still scarred by the ridges of corn planting. Our various genre stages were spread out around the farm, and in the middle of this festival grid was the Pederson homestead, a modest, remodeled farm house where Evelyn still lived, even through all the preparations leading up to the festival and those festival nights when bands pulsed their rock sounds into the early hours of the next day and campers frolicked in the dark on the land she'd tended for so long.

The amazing thing was that she didn't seem too out of place among it all. Evelyn would stop by our operations camps to greet us with warm homemade cookies and, at times, to see the commotion. It was as if she felt the need to help us or do something for the festival. Evelyn was used to hosting large groups from family gatherings to church functions, as well as feeding the farm hands. As this gathering of festival-goers was a bit more massive she probably struggled with watching the chaos before her, but her smile never dimmed.

Neither did LifeLight.

Despite the reservations from our "critics," the festival didn't seem to mind setting up on a farmstead that was active just 12 months prior to the event. The kids walked between stages like they'd always heard music bounce off the curved half-cylinder Quonset buildings, and they camped in these former fields as if they had been reclaimed as KOA campgrounds. The move was virtually seamless—at least to those who weren't there when the preparations were being made.

At the end of our first festival in the new home, the rock group MercyMe graced the main stage by leading a crowd of about 80,000 people in an a cappella version of "Amazing Grace." The sound of all those voices singing together lifted off the farmstead in a way that felt like a small taste of what Heaven must be like. The sing-along was so buoyant and charged that people 12-miles away at the convenience store off a nearby interstate exit to the south of us could hear the singing.

It was a worthy christening.

■ ■ ■

Our new festival home was the big news that year, but it might not have been the most significant thing our ministry experienced in 2010. Aside from making our big move, we also held a festival in Pakistan.

Yes, that Pakistan.

Hosting a Christian music festival in a country that is officially named The Islamic Republic of Pakistan, a place that's become synonymous with anti-American rhetoric, wasn't a goal that was itchin' to get crossed off my life's list of things to do. But when God calls we listen, and back in 2009 we were literally called to expand into Pakistan.

It started with a phone call from Pastor Rasheed, who led a Christian evangelical ministry in Pakistan. He said he had heard about LifeLight while attending a seminar in Portland put on by Luis Palau. Pastor Rasheed was calling to invite me to come to Karachi, Pakistan's most populated city of more than 23 million people, and preach the Gospel through our festival model.

For several months my response was an emphatic, "I don't think so." Festival ministry in Muslim-dominated countries had never crossed my mind before. Besides, we don't just say yes to everything or everywhere we are invited; we weigh how it feels to us, how it lines up with our given circumstances and, most of all, how it fits into God's word.

As we prayed about the issue, God's words seemed to be telling us to accept Pastor Rasheed's request.

Now, you have to understand that Pastor Rasheed is an unassuming man; yet, he's someone who is very true to Pakistani culture. He isn't an outlier trying to use the brand of Christ as a contrary angle to life in his homeland. A former professional cricket player from some years back, he had a dramatic conversion to Christianity. After attending Bible College in the United States, he returned to his home country with a passion to go all over his nation reaching out to the poor and preaching the Good News of Jesus. It was moving to hear his enthusiasm and conviction of belief to spread the Good Word throughout his south Asian nation. He wanted LifeLight to help make that happen.

Aside from making our big move, we also held a festival in Pakistan.

Yes, that Pakistan.

But before we committed to launching the festival in Pakistan, we flew Pastor Rasheed to South Dakota so he could experience the LifeLight festival firsthand. Seeing our process and how this amount of music and faith could affect such a mass of people only further convinced Pastor Rasheed that we should come to Pakistan and use the festival model in his home country.

Then, as I got to know Pastor Rasheed, his story convinced us that we needed to make that journey into the Muslim country.

His life had been difficult—he had lost a child and his wife, who was also his partner in ministry. Pastor Rasheed is a Godly man with a deep prayer life; it was probably his humble prayers which finally reached my heart to say yes to his plea.

Throughout our process of developing the Karachi festival, Vicki had never felt the desire to go to Pakistan—at all. This concerned her as everyone in the "inner circle" was convinced this was a mission we had to take; yet, Vicki didn't feel like the Holy Spirit was pulling her toward Pakistan. The fact that she had no desire to go bothered her slightly since she always wanted to go on mission trips and to new places. Still, she couldn't get past the feeling that she should pass up this opportunity.

It was a curious situation, but one that felt more assured

once our youngest daughter Rachelle came to me expressing her desires for herself and her husband Josh to join us in Karachi. There was just one problem—she couldn't bring her young daughter along. And who would watch her...that was assuming that Vicki made the trip. Funny how things work out sometimes, huh? When Vicki found out that Rachelle desired to go to Pakistan, she immediately knew why she didn't feel the pull to go herself. Her ministry was to care for her granddaughter so Rachelle could go without worries.

With our team roster set, we made the plans for the festival to take place in April of 2010. We had prayed and prepared, but we still had some anxiety about becoming some of the most obvious outsiders in a city that's no stranger to those "most dangerous cities in the world" lists. Although, to hear Pastor Rasheed talk, there was nothing to worry about. In fact, he said he knew some people in the local government who would welcome us.

We had prayed and prepared, but we still had some anxiety about becoming some of the most obvious outsiders in a city that's no stranger to those "most dangerous cities in the world" lists.

One week before we were to leave, our visas were denied entry into the country by the Pakistani government. This was after we had been assured by Pastor Rasheed, as well as the consulate, that everything was in order and we were set to make the trip. The rejection was devastating. We had already spent $30,000 dollars in preparations, but beyond the money, it was frustrating to have this developing dream suddenly dashed by bureaucracy. Still, it wasn't a complete shock. We were dealing with the Islamic Republic of Pakistan. Granting access to an American Christian ministry proclaiming the Gospel and doing mission work was not at the top of their priority list.

And trying to fix this via phone wasn't getting us any closer to Karachi, so we prayed for the right person at the consulate's office to physically take our passports and grant our entry. Like a divine appointment right on queue, I was finally able to talk to a person who understood our mission and was able to physically walk our case to each department that was needed to keep things moving to get us into the country. This was a miraculous coincidence that someone who was one of Pakistan's rare believers in Christ worked in the Islamic consulate office and happened to be the one person who could repair our visa issues. I call that a God thing.

I call that a God thing.

The day before we were to board the plane toward Pakistan, our visa problems were solved. God's divine hand had once again directed us to where He needed His message to be heard outside the church walls.

The festivals in Pakistan became a turning point for the LifeLight ministry as we saw the power of preaching Christ to an oppressed people, many of whom had never heard the truth of the Gospel before. But it was also a reaffirming moment for many of us in the ministry as it reminded us of the singular importance of God's original direction for LifeLight: to take the church outside the building's walls. Through the years this central message of our ministry had been talked about and prayed upon so many times that it could become rhetoric of sort, the kind of thing that you say over and over again to a choir of followers without giving much thought to the true meaning. But as we spread the message to these people in Pakistan, the necessity of this mantra reinvigorated us with the power of its purpose as thousands of people surrendered their lives to Christ as His hand protected us from the dangers that surrounded us there.

■ ■ ■

Now, you have to realize that when we brought the "festival" to Pakistan we didn't arrive with stages, large PA systems, and an arsenal of rock bands selling their music alongside T-shirts and posters. Our role in Pakistan was often more in line with our previous mission trips than the festival setting we had grown in southeastern South Dakota.

Those Pakistani "festivals" consisted of a medical clinic in which basic services like vitamins and medical supplies were given out as people were checked for ailments and advised on how to maintain healthy habits. We sponsored a soccer ball ministry in partnership with our friends Torrey and Heather of The Mission Ball, an organization that hands out soccer balls covered with important scriptures like the Ten Commandments and verses explaining God's plan of salvation.

The crowd was mesmerized by the music—that universal language transcending culture and language and religious barriers.

We did migrate a couple of the "festival" standards to Pakistan. I spoke through a translator to the crowds that gathered around us, along with my friend and fellow evangelist, Bret, who shared his story of tragedy, suffering, and rebirth after a motorcycle accident. His words connected with the people in a culture who knew plenty about hardship. And, of course, we had to bring some of the music that had always been central to the LifeLight festival setting.

The tunes came courtesy my daughter and her band Rachelle Hope. They played praise and pop music from their hearts and watched as the crowd was mesmerized by the music—that universal language transcending culture and language and religious barriers. While my daughter would sing "Hosanna" in English, the crowd would harmonize back and sing the chorus along with her. It was a moving experience to be a part of. As I took a moment to simply look at what we were doing in this foreign land, I was warmed by the honor and privilege of sharing God's message with these people on a field in Pakistan. When I walked on stage after the band had ended, I could feel the welcomed attention and anticipation of the crowd that was ready to hear the claims of Jesus and the hope He could bring.

We heard the sudden sound of distant gunfire.

After three nights in Karachi, we moved about two hours northeast to the city of Hyderabad. This time our movements were escorted by a security detail that guided us through the region.

During the festival's concert the crowd in this smaller city was reacting much differently than the people in Karachi had done. Even though they were listening to the music and the Good News of Christ, they were much more subdued. Later, as Bret was speaking, we heard the sudden sound of distant gunfire.

I spun around and pointed my concerned stare into Pastor Rasheed's eyes. He just gave me a reassuring nod and said, "It's OK...just a wedding celebration or something in the distance. Not a problem; keep going." So we did.

I can't lie; I was scared. Later, we were told that the gunfire we had heard was not a wedding celebration but possibly warnings for us to leave.

We gathered and prayed after the concert and some of the group lobbied for us to return to Karachi that night, even though we had planned for another night of the festival in Hyderabad. Even the ever-positive Pastor Rasheed suggested we cut the festival short and get back to Karachi. That spoke volumes to me, so we returned to Karachi the next morning, cutting our Hyderabad festival short.

During our time in Pakistan, more than 5,000 people indicated a decision to follow Christ. For many who would have identified themselves as culturally Muslim, this was a brand new path, and there would be certain consequences to their newfound allegiance to Jesus. Those who went public with their faith could risk losing their jobs, which were provided by mostly Muslim employers. For others, the devotion to Christ could mean being cut off from family and friends. Some could even experience outright, public persecution.

While there are Christian churches in Pakistan, many of them are historic carryovers, faith centers that have been grandfathered in, so to speak. They are allowed to exist though the Pakistani government would prefer to keep their messages inside the walls. The faithful must decide between standing for Christ publicly or remaining an undercover Christian in an oppressive religious state.

During our time in Pakistan, more than 5,000 people indicated a decision to follow Christ.

We weren't the only people interested in this juxtaposition of faith.

While I was speaking during our Pakistani festivals, I noticed some camera guys in the crowd during our festival in Karachi who kept moving about and getting video footage. They were clearly foreign, much like ourselves. In the busyness of the night I lost sight of them and once the festival was over they were gone.

After returning to Karachi, we were having breakfast at our hotel when a guy walked over and introduced himself to me as part of that camera crew. He was a field producer from Italy who was overseeing a crew of British TV journalists who were filming a documentary about Christians living in Pakistan. He wanted to include us in the report.

Coincidence? Hardly. This was God's divine hand directing people for His purposes. When you step out in faith in His name and take the message outside the walls of the Church He moves in very visible ways. A church with walls would never have witnessed a genesis of believers in such a place. A church without walls will pour God's love in places and circumstances you could never have envisioned.

When you step out in faith in His name and take the message outside the walls of the Church He moves in very visible ways.

■ ■ ■

Returning from Pakistan, our passion for the purpose of LifeLight had been recharged to a state not felt in quite a while. It was a good thing, because we didn't have just one festival to plan for that year. We would also be staging another in Bethany, Missouri.

It's not rare for people from various pockets of the U.S. to trek to the LifeLight festival, feel inspired by all that it entails, and take home with them a desire to bring LifeLight to their part of the world. That was the case with Mike and Tricia from Missouri. Having met us years earlier, they traveled to Sioux Falls to faithfully serve at the festival with no expectations. Eventually, they wanted a festival on their land to impact their home community, which is one of the poorest counties in all of the Show Me State. Aside from having strong faith and a good work ethic, they also have something most people with festival dreams don't—an existing Christian campground that's quite suitable for the festival experience. Tricia's parents had stopped in the LifeLight office one day and shared with us about their heart for a festival as well as the work they had been doing in Haiti. They offered to host our staff for a little retreat so we could come visit their Miracle Hills Ranch and see the cabins, activities, pool with water slides, and most importantly, the wide-open fields. They knew we would fall in love with the location as well as their hearts for ministry. They were right.

That first year in Bethany we brought a miniaturized version of the festival with a few bands and speakers. We also brought our legacy of rain as the festival endured a downpour, but persevered through it thanks to the passion and dedication of the volunteers. Through it all, we were shown the divine hand of God as so many people who could have never afforded to buy tickets for themselves or their family were able to experience the music and message—just like church, without the barriers.

Near the end of the festival, just as the closing band, Leeland, was about to perform, a security volunteer let me know there was an incident his team was watching. Someone of Asian descent had showed up at this festival, which was in the middle of rural America, via taxi. Nobody in Bethany took cabs. I'm not even sure the city of 3,000 people had a taxi service. It was rather odd, but what caught their attention was the backpack this person was wearing. She walked over near the cross by the prayer tent, placed it on the ground, and left it there. I can only imagine where these security guys' minds were going and how sweaty their palms were as they made the decision to pick up the seemingly abandoned backpack and carry it off to a field some

300 yards away. My, how our assumptions can get us into trouble.

After Leeland finished its rousing set the young lady went to the cross at the prayer tent and asked where her backpack was. Then she told her story…

She had stumbled across the Bethany LifeLight festival on the Internet and planned a trip from Japan to the U.S. with two goals in mind. The first, to see Niagara Falls; the other, to attend the LifeLight Festival in Missouri. She said she had laid her backpack down by the cross to worship to the music, assuming her backpack and items would be safe there by the cross and prayer tent. She was of Buddhist descent but found an interest here and was drawn to this event. It was a lesson and an inspiration to the prayer and security teams and to us all.

I don't know the rest of this Japanese woman's story, but one day, I want to meet her and hope to see her in heaven.

16

Taking it to Texas

While I was writing an early draft of this book we made another move. Though, this one doesn't involve the festival, just my family and I. We sold our home of 18 years—the place where the LifeLight ministry was started, the place with the barn that housed our first office, the same place that provided me the humbling lesson after falling from the rafters. It's where we watched our daughters grow alongside this ministry. This had been a home of dreams imagined and fulfilled, and yet it was clear it was time to move.

We always said when God wanted us to give it up we would. But saying that is one thing, doing it is another. We knew with our growing ministry obligations and mission work that we would be spending less and less time at our home base. Two of our daughters had married and moved out; it was time to downsize to be more mobile and ready for God's next assignment. So, we left our beloved acreage and moved into Sioux Falls, just blocks from the LifeLight office.

There were moments of sadness during the transition, but as work in the ministry picked up, we knew that God had our best interests in mind by helping us let go of a home that required a lot of time to maintain.

Through that move we learned that God is always doing a new thing—right this second, not five minutes ago, not five years in the future. He's in all places, but He designed us to be in the now, and He is in the here and now with us.

In 2013 we completed five festivals within one year—in South Dakota, Guatemala, Haiti, Texas, and Missouri. Each was different, showcasing unique local cultures and styles, yet there was the one constant: we were having a party in Jesus' name to glorify God outside the temple's walls. God works through mass evangelism and when the community comes together in unity and proclaims the truth of Jesus, miraculous things happen. As it so often seems, these miracles can start with a simple phone call.

God is always doing a new thing—right this second, not five minutes ago, not five years in the future.

One day in 2011 such a call came from Al Denson. I had remembered Al from his work years earlier in the Christian music scene of the '80s and '90s when his solo career spawned several Christian radio hits. He had won Song of the Year, had several Dove Award nominations, and had been recently inducted into the Christian Music Hall of Fame. We had met briefly in 2007 during a Christian conference in Nashville, so the call wasn't totally out of the blue, though it was far from expected.

He first asked me to put Vicki on the phone as well and then he said to us, "I want you to pray about having a LifeLight festival in Texas, on my ranch."

What?

It was one of those surprises that does more than just cause you to shake the head.

We weren't thinking about Texas. And we didn't really know how to duplicate this thing that was happening in South Dakota. We just prayed for divine appointments, and that's how the festival had spread to Missouri and Pakistan. We guess that maybe this call was one of those divine appointments, so we thought we ought to listen to Al's proposal.

The call was curious because we had also been told by a very wise Christian businessman a few months previously that we should tell our story of "Taking the church outside the walls" in Dallas. The businessman went on to say that all over the nation young people were not attending church on a regular basis, yet they managed to show up to the LifeLight festivals.

We told him that we appreciated his compliments, but we didn't know anyone in Dallas. Even if we wanted to go to Texas, we would not know where to start.

Then Al called with an apparent message of serendipity.

"My ranch is just an hour or so north of Dallas," Al said. "It is perfect for a festival, and in fact, has been used in the past for other conferences and events. I am calling you because I believe God has told me to call you. I think a LifeLight festival offered free of admission is what is needed here. Please come down and walk the grounds and pray about it. The land will be free for you to use as long as you want to do a festival there."

This seemed to be a message from God, and a familiar one, yet Vicki and I were nervous. How would we assemble a team in Texas with no budget to do so? How would we stretch and convince our staff to do even more? But most important, what was God saying we should do?

I'm sure God felt about us the same way He describes His followers in the Bible. Oh, you of little faith. It's a good thing He is a persistent God.

We did fly down to visit Al's ranch, and we brought along our dear friends and Chairman of our Board, Tom and his wife Pamela. As we walked the grounds, it was hard not to be influenced by the sheer beauty of the location that included a picturesque pond, mature trees, rolling hills, and accommodating guesthouses. It was beautiful. Al welcomed us with gratitude and a support system that helped us feel more comfortable with the task of growing the first LifeLight festival in the Lone Star state.

The thought of that task became a little easier after meeting Ann, who lived in the area and had contacted us after hearing about this new endeavor. She came to us with hopes of volunteering and shared her resume. We soon realized that with this woman's experienced leadership skills she could be a future LifeLight Texas coordinator, someone who could be a liaison to the communities of the Sherman area.

And talking to the locals, the area needed more than a liaison. They needed Jesus.

As a law enforcement officer for Texas' Grayson County told me, "I think meth and drugs are going to destroy this county; we need something to reach and rescue our youth."

There was great need in Texas for spreading God's message outside the church and there was an open invitation—two factors that rarely come together so neatly packaged.

After a second trip to the ranch with our leadership team we decided to make this step of faith deep into the heart of Texas.

The LifeLight Texas festival happened Memorial Day weekend in 2013, and like so many of its predecessors, the festival was welcomed with a bevy of challenges ranging from finances to more inopportune weather to lofty expectations.

Historically, we started our festivals small, growing them year-to-year by adding more bands, better bands, and complimentary features like specialized stages or worship tents. But in a large metropolitan area like Dallas-Fort Worth, starting small felt rather underwhelming. So we went big. But one of the problems with going big is that you need a big budget to make it happen. And, from the start, fundraising for LifeLight Texas was difficult. Everyone we spoke with wanted us to come, and they were excited about the ministry potential, but money was tight. Money is always tight for a first-year startup festival. But part of our problem was that the community of Sherman never seemed to fully jump on board with the festival. Sure, a few churches from the area gave unselfishly, as did a few faithful businesses and individuals, but most couldn't contribute. We fell well short of our budget needed to make this festival happen.

It's a good thing He is a persistent God.

Then we had to deal with the issue of timing.

The Boston Marathon bombing happened one month before LifeLight Texas, which meant the authorities in Sherman became very concerned about security issues that didn't seem to exist two months prior. Suddenly, trying to cut through the bureaucratic red tape to get the necessary assembly permits took exponentially more time than we had planned, which resulted in our staff spending less time engaged in actual ministry. Also, just to the North, across the border in Oklahoma, a community had just recently been hit by a devastating tornado.

Birthing that Texas festival was an arduous task. Then, as we delivered this new baby, it was welcomed to the world with a persistent rainstorm that lasted the three days of the festival.

But as I stood on the stage and saw the thousands of people who showed up for the inaugural year we knew God was present as we witnessed lives changing by accepting Jesus.

The thing about a festival is even if you know that God is working by His Spirit to change lives you may never hear the stories of impact. But in Texas, in the middle of the festival when I was physically sick and our team was drained from fighting rain and the slippery clay ground, a musician friend reported back to us that he had shared the love of Christ with a young man who was contemplating suicide just that day. He told the musician that he was coming to the festival to say goodbye to some of his friends. But, the music drew him in and spoke Truth to his heart. The young man said no to the enemy and said yes to God!

But God will move Heaven and earth to get to His one lost sheep.

When our team heard that story, we knew why we were in Texas. And we knew why the enemy was throwing so many challenges our way. But God will move Heaven and earth to get to His one lost sheep. We have heard many stories of contemplated or even attempted suicide as the lost have cried out for a Savior. And with each one person who surrenders to God, we rejoice! They are the ones that He came for, that He charged us to seek out.

As the Newsboys closed out the festival while singing "God's Not Dead," you could see the evidence of it in the crowd gathered in the heart of Texas.

17

To God be the Glory

Again, Jesus spoke to them, saying, "I am the light of the world. Whoever follows me will not walk in darkness, but will have the light of life." John 8:12

That is the verse that God gave our small group of eight many years ago, the verse that launched a ministry and a new journey with God.

LifeLight started out small. Very small, in fact. It started with concerts reaching just a hundred people or so. While we loved promoting concerts, it was such a small piece of this huge picture that God had placed in our hearts—so huge that He didn't always show us parts of it until we were ready.

Our call has taken us from promoting those small music concerts to leading mission trips around the world, and the core of it has been an unlikely, massive music festival in the plains of South

Dakota. How did this all happen so quickly?

By saying, "Yes."

All throughout our journey we have witnessed miracles of God's divine guidance and His use of ordinary people to facilitate His extraordinary work. God can use anyone. He used me. He used my wife. He used our children. He used so many faithful friends and volunteers. And, God has used the LifeLight experience as a way for many average people to get into ministry. God called, and they answered. The point is—God can use anyone, if we are available and obedient.

He can use our qualifications, education, talents, heritage, and background, but He doesn't need any of those things.

He just needs us to accept His plan and our place in it.

Granted, accepting the idea that God will take care of us as we walk into the unknown can be difficult to embrace—even for believers. The LifeLight story is an example that the faithful will be watched over. Or, if you'd like a different example, take the Apostle Paul from the Bible; though he was well-educated, he said that he came to people determined to know nothing except Christ and Christ crucified. He came in weakness, fear, and trembling so that people's faith might not rest in the wisdom of men, but in the power of God.

He can use our qualifications, education, talents, heritage, and background, but He doesn't need any of those things.

If Paul, the Apostle who Jesus appointed to bring the message outside of Jerusalem and to be the writer of a good portion of the New Testament, stepped into his journey with God with some fear, then there's no shame in feeling the same. God can use us if we will let Him.

Sometimes His answers have not been, and are not, what we

choose, but that's what walking with Him means, trusting.

Trust God in all things. Obey God in all things.

There are many people in humble circumstances walking with God every day and their plans and dreams have not worked out as they envisioned. God is still with them and perhaps their stories of faith are the greater example of faith and trust—no matter what. Faith involves being obedient to God no matter how it looks, trusting that He will finish the good work He started.

Trust God in all things.
Obey God in all things.

From our music festival in Middle America to the fields of Ethiopia to the streets of Karachi, Pakistan, there is a common thread where God has moved and drawn people to Himself. The festivals have been a place where people have laid down their own agendas for the sake of proclaiming the Gospel, and where churches have partnered and worked together despite their differences.

That has been God's prevailing purpose with LifeLight, to take the Church outside the walls to proclaim the Gospel to all who will hear it.

Though, when you're spreading the will of God across the world, sometimes you have to remember to hear God's voice for yourself—even when it seems distant, or silent, for great periods of time. He is there. And He can always be found in the Bible; it's where I've realized He is always waiting for me. And, through His word, I know He will guide LifeLight wherever He wants to take it. That's what He's always done. And I have continued to follow, praying that we will be found faithful in the end; that we will finish well the work He has called us to do.

If there's been a formula for our ministry, it has been this: praise Him with music, proclaim His words, and watch Him work.

Sounds a lot like church, huh?

One day Jesus is coming back for His Church and that is the hope we have as believers. It will be a glorious day! Bigger than any festival or gathering here on Earth. Until that day we will keep celebrating His name and proclaiming His message to the one and to the masses.

Praise Him with music, proclaim His words, and watch Him work.

His message is simple, by surrendering to Jesus (not a religion), confessing and repenting of our own sin, accepting His sacrifice of shed blood on the cross, and trusting in Him alone for salvation, we become a Child of God and are given eternal life. We should then long to become more like Him and seek a life of holiness and obedience that is pleasing to Him.

Early in my life I was questioning the Church and its relevancy in reaching the un-churched masses of people. Now I believe it was me who God was convicting to live what I was being called to. His overarching question was, “Alan, what are you doing about it?” It became my burden too.

I love the Church. I have grown up in church, and it has been where I have spent most of my life. It’s where I’m comfortable, and yet God has made me conscious of the people outside the walls.

It became our ministry’s mission to reach those people. It just so happens that God’s design meant we would be using music to bring them toward His message.

There are a variety of wonderful churches with many different styles of worship that teach God’s word. LifeLight’s ultimate goal, by taking the church outside the walls, is to eventually see people come inside the walls to be engaged with the body of believers.

I hope those outside the walls will not prejudge with thoughts like, “The church is full of hypocrites,” or, “I hate organized religion."

Yes, there are hypocrites in the Church, but there are hypocrites everywhere—in sports, business, politics, and in life in general.

We are all flawed and will disappoint each other, but God will not disappoint you.

To those plugged into the Church, think about those around you and how you might be a blessing. Your pastor's primary role is to train and equip you to reach them. The world will not be won to Christ by the "paid professionals" alone. It is up to you, and I, to be the light of life to those people God has put around us. He is working in and through people like you and I to reach others, help heal their hurts, and be part of changing the darkness of this world with the Light of Christ—the Church running as God designed it can always accomplish great things.

I'd like to leave you with a little story from Pastor Jesse Wilson that I picked up somewhere along the way that I like to retell now and again.

In this tale a group of angels had gathered around the Lord Jesus Christ after He had come back from Earth—the first time. They were asking Him questions, and one angel said, "Lord, how are you going to spread the Gospel message throughout the world?"

Well, Jesus said, "I have called out disciples to carry out my great commission. They will go and share this wonderful message with others who will respond, and they in turn will go and share with others who need to be saved."

LifeLight's ultimate goal, by taking the church outside the walls, is to eventually see people come inside the walls to be engaged with the body of believers.

The angel replied, "Are you telling me that you have entrusted the task of getting out the message of eternal life and salvation—the greatest news in all of creation—to those earthlings, counting on them to be witnesses to the Gospel message and to take it around the world?"

The Lord Jesus affirmed, "That's absolutely right."

The angel looked at Him with a face of worry and doubt.

"Well, Lord, what if they don't do what you command them to do? What is Plan B?"

The Lord replied, "There is no Plan B."

There is no Plan B.

The overarching lesson of the LifeLight journey is about saying yes, stepping forward, and forgetting about an alternate or backup plan. There is no real Plan B. It really is about trusting in God completely and walking it out in our everyday lives.

Step out in faith. Bring light into darkness. Take the Church outside the walls. Be the Church to the hurting world that is waiting to hear from you.

Go be the Light of Life.

To God be the Glory

GET LIFE

Get Life–How to Know God

The Bible says we can know God through a relationship with His Son, Jesus Christ.

- John 17:3 "Now this is eternal life: that they may know You, the only true God, and Jesus Christ, whom You have sent."

Not only are we promised eternal life through knowing Christ, but the joy of knowing God starts now. The life of a Christian may not always be easy, but God through His Spirit will be with you always. And once you are adopted as a child of God, you are promised eternal life. You can have that assurance.

- John 1:12 "Yet to all who received Him, to those who believed in His name, He gave the right to become children of God."
- I John 5:11-13 "And this is the testimony: God has given us eternal life, and this life is in His Son. He who has the

Son has life; he who does not have the Son of God does not have life. I write these things to you who believe in the name of the Son of God so that you may know that you have eternal life."

Want to know God and have a relationship with Him? You can do that now. It's this simple:

First—Realize you are a sinner…the Bible says none of us are good enough, and we can't earn our way to Heaven.

- Romans 3:10 "As it is written: There is no one righteous, not even one."
- Romans 3:23 "…for all have sinned and fall short of the glory of God…"

Second—Acknowledge that Jesus died on the cross for you.

- Romans 5:8 "But God demonstrates His own love for us in this: While we were still sinners, Christ died for us."
- 1 John 1:7 "But if we walk in the light, as He is in the light, we have fellowship with one another, and the blood of Jesus, His Son, purifies us from all sin."

Third—Be willing to turn from your sin and change direction. Instead of running from God…run toward Him. The Bible calls this repentance.

- Acts 3:19 "Repent, then, and turn to God, so that your sins may be wiped out, that times of refreshing may come from the Lord."

Fourth—Receive Jesus into your life. It's not about reciting a creed or just going to church. It's having Jesus Christ Himself take residence in your life.

- Revelation 3:20 "I stand at the door of your heart and

knock. If anyone hears my voice and opens the door, I will come in."

- Romans 10:9-10 "If you confess with your mouth that Jesus is Lord and believe in your heart that God raised Him from the dead, you will be saved. For with the heart one believes and is justified, and with the mouth one confesses and is saved."

Finally—Tell Him. Pray this prayer:

Lord Jesus, I know that I am a sinner...I know that You died for my sins and rose again from the dead. Right now I turn from my sins and open the door of my heart and my life to You. I want You to be Lord and Master. Jesus, I fully surrender to You. Amen.

First, if you sincerely prayed this from your heart, let someone know and email us at Office@LifeLight.org. We would love to help you in your journey!

Next, find a church that presents God's Word as the infallible truth and seek out a group of Christians who want to explore the Bible together. For resources or help, please do not hesitate to contact the LifeLight office at Office@LifeLight.org.

Alan and Vicki Greene

About the Author

Alan Greene is pursuing God's call on his life by taking the Church outside the walls. His heart to unify the body of Christ to reach the lost is what motivates him. With the conviction of an evangelist and his background of both ministry and business experience, he's been given a broad perspective on the calling of the Church today.

Alan speaks at churches, events, and conferences on the call of the Church and uniting Christians centered on God's word. He sits on the Cabinet of Next Generation Alliance, a network of evangelists started by the Luis Palau Association and was ordained through the American Evangelistic Association. His passion is to share the Gospel message with as many people as possible and encourage the ongoing work of evangelism and missions in fulfilling Acts 1:8.

Alan and his wife Vicki are the founders of LifeLight Communications. They are the proud parents of three beautiful daughters and blessed grandparents of their wonderful grandchildren.

While they reside in Sioux Falls, SD, Alan and Vicki enjoy traveling the country and world, spreading the Gospel of Jesus Christ wherever they go.

LifeLight Office Headquarters

About LifeLight

LifeLight Communications, Inc. is a 501(c)(3) non-profit Evangelistic Proclamation Organization. We view ourselves as missionaries and base our work from Acts 1:8, "You will receive power when the Holy Spirit has come upon you, and you will be my witnesses in Jerusalem and in all Judea and Samaria, and to the end of the earth." We exist to proclaim the Gospel through music and the message.

While on a mission trip to Mexico in 1998, God grabbed ahold of Alan Vicki's hearts with the mission of "Taking the Church outside the Walls." What started out as a festival on a church lawn has now grown into an international ministry involving many who have a heart to reach people with the Gospel. In John 8:12 Jesus said, "I am the light of the world. Whoever follows me will not walk in darkness but will have the Light of Life." From this verse the ministry of LifeLight was born.

LifeLight's founding principle is to offer all festivals free of admission so that ALL may come and ALL may hear the Gospel message. The LifeLight festival, while the most visible, is one of three areas of LifeLight's ministry: festivals, missions, and outreach. Yet LifeLight is ONE ministry with ONE mission, "Taking the Church outside the walls, bringing Light into the darkness with the life-changing message of the Gospel of Jesus Christ."

LifeLight Communications Inc. is located in Sioux Falls, SD.

To book Alan Greene as a speaker,
contact LifeLight at Office@LifeLight.org
or 605-338-2847.

To learn more about the ministry of LifeLight,
visit www.LifeLight.org.

LifeLight

TAKING THE CHURCH
OUTSIDE THE WALLS

IN PICTURES

They Ran

A Permanent Festival Home

Mexico Missions

Love Ethiopia Festival

Aerial of WWW Water Park

Miracle Babies

Grandchildren Blessings

LifeLight Office Headquarters

SD Festival Crowd

Life
Light
John 8:12

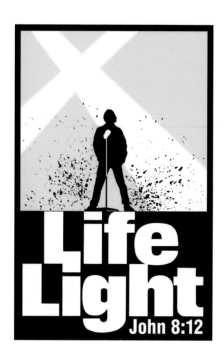